THE
Offline Dating
METHOD

THE *Offline Dating* METHOD

HOW TO ATTRACT
A GREAT GUY
IN THE
Real World

CAMILLE VIRGINIA

Dedication

To my parents, who've supported and encouraged me
through every step of this incredible adventure.

Reviews and Praise

"The Offline Dating Method is **cleverly disguised as a dating book**…but it's actually **a witty manifesto on how to master the art of meaningful connection** while living in a tech-obsessed culture. Readers will not only get the power to date in the real world, they'll also live a more fulfilling life."
    – Sonya, client

"You don't have to be sensitive, shy or socially awkward to get A TON out of Camille's material. I found her less than a year ago and I've already gotten maybe **12 dates, 2 new clients, vendor leads and some fun friends** JUST because of her tips on how to be approachable."
    – Dr. Cari O'Neal

"Camille's 'offline dating' perspective is so unique. She starts with the tiniest step to get you comfortable with strangers by treating everyone as if you're already friends with them. Then the Empathic Listening Technique where **a real connection is the foundation of getting asked out**. The exercises help you reflect on the barriers that might be holding you back, which is powerful. **I did get ask-outs using Camille's method**. But more importantly, her method helps me have fewer doubts, anxiety, and fears when I show up at parties/events/new gyms by myself."
    – Zenna, client

"This book is so full of wisdom! It's **practical, insightful, and awesome**. I especially loved 'Dress for Confidence and a Conversation' – wow… Camille really drove it home on the importance of dressing nicely!"
    – Allie, client

"The Offline Dating Method is a brilliant testament to the power of starting a relationship off in person vs. online. Being able to draw upon all your senses in order to really 'know' someone is critical, especially in a day and age when we communicate less than ever. **This book is powerful, engaging, and even as a happily married woman, I could not put this down.** The lessons I learned can be applied to any interaction with any human. I also loved the reminder to always be curious. People are complex and fascinating, and if you keep your mind open and ask questions and sincerely show interest in others, you will be rewarded with some of the loveliest gifts through connection that you could imagine."
  – Melody, advanced reader

"This book is right on the mark for smart, single women who are not interested in frivolous relationships - who want a partner and want to expand their social circle. The book is well researched and organized, with a pile of thought put into it. Most importantly **it provides answers for how to become more confident and self-aware.**"
  – Jeff, advanced reader

"Even though I'm 67, and now happily married, this book was perfect for me. I found so many insights on how to **increase the quality of my relationships with everyone - including my husband!** Camille is very authentic and has a clever, enjoyable sense of humor. She spells the tips out clearly, gives specific examples, and made the book very reader-friendly and interactive. The quotes alone show how much research was put into the book. It was a joy to read, twice!"
  – Zelda, advanced reader

"If you want to get into a really positive place about dating, this is for you. Camille is charming, with great ideas, extensive content, wonderful energy – but above all, **you feel empowered and with a fresh look at how to be around men.**"
  – Eleanor, workshop student

*"Camille helps women step into their 'Once upon a time' stories, and transforms wishes of princes and gentlemen into **face-to-face conversations and meaningful dates**."*
  – Alissa Trumbull, journalist

*"Camille offered new ideas that challenged my existing beliefs about dating and being social. I had several ah-hah moments with concrete next-steps – and I came away with several deeper awarenesses for myself. **If you're interested in connecting deeper, both to self and other people**, I recommend Camille and her material."*
  – Elena, workshop student

*"People crave connection but can struggle to find it due to stories we play in our heads where we judge ourselves - or others - and then don't take action. The moment passes, and the next opportunity to connect becomes a tiny bit harder. **Camille does an exquisite job of putting her humanness, tenderness, and courage on display in her work.** I appreciate her practical tips on how to form more authentic connections with the world around me. Thank you, Camille, for your service to the world!"*
  – Louis Amoroso, Founder, Travel.Light.World

*"This book is a **conversation and dating game-changer**. I love how **this information can be applied in every culture**, as some who has used the norms of my culture/religion to hinder human connection in the love department. I also love the tactical advice on how to be present, how to be selective with the company you keep, how to be vulnerable, and most of all how to be kind to yourself."*
  – Sarah, client

Free Resources

Want an easy way to apply key tips from *The Offline Dating Method*, so you can start attracting great men as quickly as possible?

Join the FREE 3-Day Challenge…

The Offline Dating Challenge:
Three Days to a Red-Hot Date in the Real World

Go to **www.OfflineDatingMethod.com/Challenge**

The challenge follows the material in *The Offline Dating Method*, delivering chapter highlights straight to your inbox. As a bonus, you'll also get the Experiential Workbook, with exclusive exercises not found in the book, so you can fast-track your way into the arms of a great man.

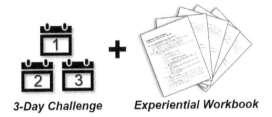

3-Day Challenge   *Experiential Workbook*

Join FREE at…
www.OfflineDatingMethod.com/Challenge

I'll see you there!

xo
Camille

Table of Contents

Introduction: Your Secret Edge Over the Apps............ 1

Chapter I: Magnetic Approachability........................... 13
Master the art of approachability to attract a great man - without saying a word

- **Results You'll Get From This Chapter**.................... 16
- **The Irresistible Woman: Authentic, Alluring, *Approachable*..17**
  - Location is Everything..18
  - Simple Social Warm-Ups 20
  - The #1 Principle of Approachability 24
  - Seven Ways to Snap Into the Present 25
- **Three Pillars of Magnetic Approachability**............ 28
  - Pillar 1: Prepping...29
  - Pillar 2: Positioning..39
  - Pillar 3: Projecting..43

Chapter II: Effortless Engagement........................... 55
Discover how to talk to any man with zero risk of rejection (even if you're shy)

- **Results You'll Get From This Chapter** 60
- **Consistency 101: Your Shift into Effortless Engagement** 65
- **If He Initiates With You**.. 77
  - The Rules of Engagement 77
- **If You Initiate With Him**....................................... 87
  - The Rules of Engagement 87
  - Overcoming the Four Fears 92
  - Eleven Super Simple Ways to Start a Conversation 99
- **How to Keep it Going – Or Shut It Down** 106

- The Four-Word Transition to Meaningful 106
- Death of a Conversation 107

• Essential Engagement Extras 109
- Four Ways to Never Forget Someone's Name Again 109
- Nine Actions to Gain Social Momentum 112
- How to Handle "One of Those Days" 119

Chapter III: Asked Out Organically **121**
Create instantly meaningful connections and inspire a great guy to ask you out

• Results You'll Get From This Chapter 125

• Warning! You'll Be a Wanted Woman 135
- How to Avoid The Catch-Up Cycle of Doom 136
- All Praise and No Action Makes Anyone a Dull Boy (or Girl).139

• The Five Elements of a Meaningful Conversation............... 140
- Element 1: Ask Awesome Questions..142
- Element 2: Hold Space for Silence 150
- Element 3: Listen Like Your Life Depends Upon It................152
- Element 4: Release Judgment 169
- Element 5: Share Insights and Stories 182

• How to Seal the Deal 199
- Here's Why It Needs to Be an Actual Date 199
- Three Ways to Get a Date with Him 200
- Script: How I Got a Date on LinkedIn 206

• More Tips for Your Conversational Arsenal 208
- Don't Say This to Him, or Anyone. Ever. 208
- How to Know When to Exit the Conversation 212
- Opportunities > Outcomes 214
- Four Ways to Recover From Forgetting a Name 216
- Instant Charm Hacks...218
- Ménage à Meaningful 220
- Tech, Interrupted 221

Conclusion: The World is Now Your Dating Playground...223

Coaching: How to Upgrade Your Support...................225

Next Books: The Sequel and The Prequel....................227

Acknowledgments: A Few Special Thank-You's........ 233

Guide: All Book Sections by Page Number.................237

Index 245

Your Secret Edge
Over the Apps

"Tinder is like a Twinkie." My client Alison was having an epiphany. "It's tempting and convenient… but full of artificial ingredients and leaves you craving something of actual substance afterward."

Like Alison, many women have had less-than-stellar experiences in the digital dating world. The journey to find love online can feel like an endless job application process filled with harassing messages, lies, and the constant sting of rejection by men you've never even met. If you haven't dabbled in the online scene yourself, chances are you've heard at least one, "Are you kidding me?" story from a single girlfriend who's tried it.

It's no wonder research has repeatedly shown that dating app use has a direct correlation to body shame and lower self-esteem.[1] Even worse, a study revealed that despite all the technology making us more "accessible" than ever, three out of four Americans struggle with loneliness.[2]

This growing epidemic of inadequacy and social isolation is devastating. However, this mass disconnection has also created a unique opportunity unlike any other in history: an untapped market of millions who are starved for face-to-face connection with each other.

Mastering the art of the real-world connection enables you to provide fulfillment to those who are craving it. **That means the power to attract the best people – including the best men – is now yours for the taking.**

---

1 "Tinder: Swiping Self Esteem?," American Psychological Association. August 4, 2016.
2 Ellen E. Lee et al., "High Prevalence and Adverse Health Effects of Loneliness in Community-Dwelling Adults Across the Lifespan," International psychogeriatrics, 2018.

Before I show you how to wield that magical attraction power, let's take a deeper look at why online dating and apps aren't working for you.

Spoiler alert: it's not you, it's them.

The Five Digital Barriers Keeping You Single

"For so many of the online daters we met in different cities, the process had morphed from something fun and exciting into a source of stress and dread."
   – Aziz Ansari, *Modern Romance*

Why does the technology that's supposed to help you meet your soulmate tend to make you feel like he's even further out of reach?

It all boils down to five key barriers that are actively preventing you from attracting your match every time you enter the online dating space…

#1 Instant Attraction, Long-Term Disappointment

Online dating and dating apps are like a "human supermarket" designed to mimic your online shopping behavior. That means many people treat others they encounter online in the same way they would in browsing for a lamp on Amazon: as a disposable commodity judged mostly by appearance. OkCupid founder, Christian Rudder, estimated that photos drive 90% of activity in online dating.[3]

#2 The Paralyzing "Paradox of Choice"

In his book *The Paradox of Choice*, author Barry Schwartz describes how having too many options can significantly decrease happiness. In the digital dating world, there are thousands of dating apps on the market – with big players like Tinder boasting an estimated 50 million members.[4] Exposing yourself to even a fraction of that number of people is enough

3 Christian Rudder, Dataclysm: Who We Are When We Think No One's Looking (New York: Crown Publishers, 2014).
4 Sarah Perez, "Tinder pilots Places, a feature that tracks your location for better matches," Tech Crunch. May 23, 2018.

to trigger "analysis paralysis," where you become so overwhelmed by choices that you're unable to make any decision at all.

#3 The House Always Wins

In addition to being modeled after addictive casino games, online dating and apps are optimized for user *engagement* (i.e. membership and advertising revenue) instead of user *desired outcome* (i.e. finding your future husband). Think about it: as soon as you find your lifelong partner the platforms lose you as a customer. And that's a risk this $1.9 billion industry is probably not willing to take.[5]

#4 The Mean Behind the Screen

Not only are online dating websites and apps designed to keep you single, they often bring out the worst behavior in people – from sexual harassment and body shaming to lying about age, appearance, and relationship status.

Interacting with someone from behind a screen makes it easier to remain anonymous and avoid any real-time repercussions – such as watching tears stream down the cheek of the woman you just insulted – that tend to happen when treating others badly in-person.[6]

Statistically, but not shockingly, the majority of the online abuse targets are female, with 70% of women describing online harassment as a major problem.[7] A recent Harvard study of 1,700 adults also revealed that people who use dating apps are more likely to have an eating disorder; particularly female users, who had 2.3 to 26.9 times higher odds of using "unhealthy weight control behaviors, possibly due to the physical appearance pressures typically associated with social media."[8]

---

5 Hayley Matthews, "27 Online Dating Statistics & What They Mean for the Future of Dating," Dating News. June 15, 2018.
6 Gaia Vince, "Evolution Explains Why We Act Differently Online," BBC. April 3, 2018.
7 Maeve Duggan, "Online Harassment 2017" (Pew Research Center, Washington, 2017).
8 Alvin Tran et al., "Dating App Use and Unhealthy Weight Control Behaviors Among a Sample of U.S. Adults: A Cross-Sectional Study," Journal of Eating Disorders 7, no. 1 (2019).

#5 Anti-Social Media

Human behavior may have adapted to the speed of modern technology, but the human need for social fulfillment has not. No wonder it's been shown that people who are addicted to social media (which inherently deprives them of time with people face-to-face) have a higher risk of suffering from depression.[9]

Humans haven't lost the need to connect. We've simply changed the ways we attempt to do it – and many would say not for the better. Even worse, with no regulations around the conglomerates who are leading the online industry, our current situation is likely to become even worse.

The good news is that it's entirely up to you whether you want to continue relying on systems that are stacked against you – or take back control by choosing a different dating approach that puts *you* in the driver's seat of your love and social life.

Note: Online dating has indeed worked for many and resulted in some happy relationships. But solely relying on these digital platforms means missing out on endless opportunities to meet the love of your life in the real world. Plus, it runs the risk of swiping away years of your life – and your soul – in the process.

The Solution is Simple

"Surrounded by digital, we now crave experiences that are more tactile and human-centric."
> – David Sax, *The Revenge of Analog*

Now that you know the cyber forces working against you, let's talk about what you can do about them.

(Hint: it's not a surface-level solution or temporary fix, such as hiring someone to re-write your online profile or getting a wardrobe makeover).

---

9 Liu Y. Lin et al., "Association Between Social Media Use and Depression Among U.S. Young Adults," Depression and anxiety 33, no. 4 (2016).

The only way to bypass the barriers is to stop relying exclusively on online platforms to meet your future partner and start attracting great men in the real world.

In the '90s, social psychologist Dr. Arthur Aron led a study which showed how certain meaningful questions were able to rapidly build emotional intimacy between two people who had never met each other.[10] The process even led to several pairs falling in love with each other!

That study is even more applicable today because meaningful connection is declining and being replaced by more transactional interactions that are void of real substance, interest, and frankly, fun.

This is where the benefits of meeting someone in-person really come into play. Being in the physical presence of another person provides you with what I call The Offline Advantage – and the secret formula behind that advantage is a phenomenon known scientifically as "cluster cues."

Cluster cues are your instinctive powers to pick up on body language, movements, tonality, and other aspects of your fellow humans. They help you instantly determine the other person's personality, current mood, trustworthiness, and whether or not they might pose a threat to you in that moment. That evaluation process all takes place in the blink of an eye - even when you aren't aware that it's happening.

But the cluster cues screening process (and, thus, The Offline Advantage) can't happen from behind a screen. Which means when you meet someone online, you're at a big disadvantage in determining crucial aspects about them – from what they actually look like, to their level of honesty, to sensing if they intend to harm to you.

Meeting someone in the real world will always have massive advantages over an algorithmic approach. Read on for seven benefits that come with The Offline Advantage...

---

10 Arthur Aron et al., "The Experimental Generation of Interpersonal Closeness: A Procedure and Some Preliminary Findings," Personality and Social Psychology Bulletin 2, no. 4 (1997).

#1 Competition is minimal

When you date online, you're competing against tens of thousands of other women – sometimes for only two seconds of a man's attention. Why subject yourself to a space where you can so easily be swiped-over? When you meet a man in the real world, you can captivate his full attention and can make a more lasting impression because you've created an actual energetic experience together.

#2 It's an instant confirmation of the basics

A recent study by eHarmony revealed that 53% of Americans aren't entirely truthful in their online profile.[11] When you're face-to-face with someone, they can't lie about what they look like or fake their social skills. In a matter of seconds, you just confirmed the basics – saving days or even weeks of emotionally investing in someone only to discover they're not who they claim to be.

#3 It saves you precious time and energy

With the average Millennial spending more than ten hours per week on dating apps, sifting through hundreds of profiles and messages each day can feel like a second full-time job.[12] Offline dating gives you the power to attract men as you simply go about your normal daily routine – from flirting with your pharmacist to getting asked out by that guy with the Dalmatian at the dog park.

#4 It's really fun

What if you could pop into the grocery store and be asked on a date in the ice cream section? Or drop by a friend's barbeque and meet your future boyfriend there? Or rendezvous with an ex to catch-up over coffee and have another man ask for your phone number right in front of him? Those are just a few of my own offline adventures, and they were so much fun!

---

11 Isabel Thottam, "10 Online Dating Statistics You Should Know (U.S.)," eHarmony, accessed August 4, 2019.
12 Jack Peat, "Millennials 'Spend 10 Hours a Week on Dating Apps'," Independent. January 23, 2018.

#5 You will be treated much better

Humans are hardwired to value the things they put effort into. Online dating and apps have become so convenient that many people don't value them, nor the people they encounter there. Being face-to-face with another person requires more risk and emotional investment, which inherently places a higher value on those interactions and naturally makes each person step-up their kindness and respect game.[13]

#6 You're more likely to find a real match

Also revealed in the eHarmony study was that only one in five committed relationships begin online.[14] Which makes sense: when you're out and about simply being your best self in the real world, you're likely to attract a man who likes you for *you* because he can instantly read into your body language, conversation skills, and other traits humans instinctively look for to assess compatibility with each other.

#7 You'll satisfy your fundamental need for connection

It's been shown that our innate need for human connection is equally as important as our basic need for food, water, and shelter[15] and that creating bonds with others can even be a powerful antidote to addiction.[16] The invention of the internet didn't erase eons of our bio-programming to seek fulfillment via connecting with each other. It simply tricked us into believing we can satisfy that need from behind a screen. When you're face-to-face with another human, you can feel their energy, read their body language, and create a deep connection that fulfills you on an essential level.

---

13 Gaia Vince, "Evolution Explains Why We Act Differently Online," BBC.
14 Thottam, "10 Online Dating Statistics You Should Know (U.S.)"
15 Matthew D. Lieberman, Social: Why Our Brains Are Wired to Connect, First edition (New York: Crown Publishers, 2013).
16 Johann Hari, "Everything You Think You Know About Addiction Is Wrong," TED Talk, June 2015.

The Journey That Led Me to You

Throughout my teen years, I was very shy – not only around men, but around *everyone*. I could barely look some people in the eye without blushing and turning away.

I finally grew tired of feeling socially clueless, so I started taking small risks to create more connections through trial and error – such as forcing myself to go places alone (scary!), sitting next to a new person at lunch, and calling my crush's house twenty times after finally working up the nerve to ask him to the homecoming dance (not recommended).

In the process, I not only found a passion for connecting with others in-person but started getting asked out by men in everyday places – like the craft store, on the train, and even at the airport. Many of those encounters turned into wonderful long-term relationships – and of course, many others were lessons on the qualities I *didn't* want in my future partner.

As online dating became more mainstream and dating apps hit the market, I continued to connect and be asked out by men in the real world. Other women started asking for the secrets behind my "offline" success and I realized luck had nothing to do with it; I was *creating* these opportunities for connection. So I put together a PowerPoint presentation titled, "How to Let Men Pick You Up," which turned into a live workshop that I ended up teaching to hundreds of single women across Chicago.

I knew, however, that I wanted to help more women than were able to attend an evening workshop. So I started my business, Master Offline Dating, which has now reached thousands of women around the world.

The Offline Dating Method gives you the invaluable advice and results I learned over all those experiences – minus the awkwardness and emotional pain I went through and in a fraction of the time it took me to discover them.

The Universal Power of Human Connection

"I am human and I need to be loved, just like everybody else does…"
— The Smiths, "How Soon is Now"

The tips in *The Offline Dating Method* are based on aspects of human behavior and desires that are hardwired deep within your DNA. That means the advice in this book works for (and on) everyone, regardless of age, race, ethnicity, sexual orientation, or gender identity.

Over the past decade, I've dated men from dozens of different professions, ranging across a fifty-year age span, from all seven continents (well, one spent a few seasons in Antarctica), as well as every major religion. I also have clients and readers from over one-hundred different countries that have applied my tips and enjoyed results in their home cultures.

What I've learned from all that is this: at the end of the day, humans are humans are humans. We are all more alike than we are different, and every one of us, on some level, wants acceptance, appreciation, and love.

This also means that you *already* have the tools to create meaningful connections and find the love of your life in the real world; they've just been buried beneath the noise of modern life and the five digital barriers.

Your Roadmap to Real-World Connection

No matter how shy or socially awkward you feel right now, *The Offline Dating Method* will show you how to attract a great guy in the real world so you can create your own happily-ever-after *and* feel fulfilled on a level you never knew existed.

Our journey through this book will have three parts…

Chapter I: Magnetic Approachability

Master the art of approachability to attract a great man - without saying a word

First, I'll show you how to catch the eye of a great guy and magnetically pull him to you without saying a word, as well as discover how to...

- Feel more socially confident and comfortable with strangers
- No longer feel invisible around men
- Avoid fear of rejection by getting men to approach you

Chapter II: Effortless Engagement

Discover how to talk to any man with zero risk of rejection (even if you're shy)

Next, I'll show you how to align your thoughts, words, and actions to put you into an effortless flow so that you can start a conversation with anyone, as well as...

- Talk to anyone with zero risk of rejection (seriously!)
- Feel in control of every conversation – including how to end it
- Build instant trust and rapport with everyone you meet

Chapter III: Asked Out Organically

Create instantly meaningful connections and inspire a great guy to ask you out

Finally, you'll learn my Five Elements of a Meaningful Conversation, my framework which leads quality men to ask you out. I'll also show you...

- How to feel energized by every conversation instead of drained
- How to quickly filter out the men who aren't right for you
- Techniques to feel instantly less lonely and more socially fulfilled

How to Avoid "Advice Overwhelm"

This book has a *ton* of tips, techniques, and resources, all delivered in bite-sized sections to help simplify concepts and make taking action as easy as possible. Refer to the *Guide: All Book Sections by Page Number* at the end of the book for a visual map of how all the topics flow together and what page you can find them on.

You also do not – I repeat, do NOT – need to apply all or even most of the tips to start seeing amazing results in your own life.

Sometimes all you need is a small shift for everything else to fall into alignment. As you go through this book, write down insights as they come to you and choose the ones that sound fun, exciting, or interesting; that's the signal that tip is meant just for you.

Creating your own custom roadmap of tips will help you feel naturally aligned as well as *enjoy* the process of meeting men. Finding the fun will inspire you to practice more, which means you'll enjoy better results.

A Special Invitation

"'Meeting your soulmate has a certain amount of meant-to-be-ness to it, AND it requires a big dose of make-it-happen-ness."
– Arielle Ford, author and personal growth leader

Throughout this book, you'll see references to The Offline Dating Method Experiential Workbook, my FREE resource to record your Action Item answers all in one place - plus these two bonuses…

Bonus #1: Dozens of Exclusive Exercises not found in the book, to help you create your own attraction action plan.

Bonus #2: The Offline Dating Challenge: 3 Days to a Red-Hot Date in the Real World, which follows the book and delivers key tips from each chapter straight to your inbox so it's easier to take action.

Grab the three gifts at…
www.OfflineDatingMethod.com/Challenge

The book stands on its own without the resources, but they're there whenever you need them to help apply the material.

Now it's time to cozy up on the couch with a comfy blanket, grab a cup of tea or glass of wine, and dive into your date with destiny in the real world!

CHAPTER I

Magnetic Approachability

*Master the art of approachability
to attract a great man -
without saying a word*

Mastering the art of approachability gives you the power to attract men like a magnet, *without saying a word*.

Humans are social creatures, which means we intrinsically feel fulfilled by being around other humans. In this chapter section, *Chapter I: Magnetic Approachability,* we'll focus on boosting your social comfort level using natural cues and reveal authentic techniques that will magnetically draw the right people to you.

(I'll show you what to say to them in the next section, *Chapter II: Effortless Engagement,* and how to turn that conversation into a date in *Chapter III: Asked Out Organically.*)

But before jumping into approachability tips, you must clear a hurdle that's likely been tripping up your ability to create a connection in the real world.

The never-ending battle for your attention

Your attention is pulled in a million different directions every day, which means even when you're out and about you're likely "tuned out" in some way, in an attempt to cope with it all – from a pop-up ad on an online article to the bad driver who just cut you off on the freeway.

Maybe you love listening to your favorite podcast while on your weekly grocery store run. Or call your mom every morning while walking the dog. Or use your lunch breaks to check-in over text with your BFF about how things are going with her new man.

All of these actions make it hard to notice the other people around you, let alone create an actual connection with them.

....

Technology may provide endless ways to contact each other, but it can never fulfill your need for human connection.

....

Simple daily habits to attract men like a magnet

The good news is, once you know how, it's quite easy to engage other people on a meaningful level.

The goal of becoming more approachable is to get you into the state of Magnetic Approachability, where you're as comfortable and confident in the company of strangers as you are sitting on your couch at home curled up with the latest copy of *People Magazine*.

To put it in scientific terms, only after you reach a certain level of feeling socially secure can you then move on to the next levels in Maslow's Hierarchy of Needs: Love and Belonging (e.g. conversation and inclusion, which we'll cover in Chapter II) and Self-Esteem (e.g. connection with yourself and others, which I'll show you how to master in Chapter III).

Maslow's Hierarchy of Needs

Self-Actualization
morality, problem solving, creativity, lack of prejudice

Self-Esteem
self-confidence, respect of others

Love and Belonging
friendship, family, intimacy, sense of connection

Safety and Security
security of body, employment, resources, health, property

Physiological
air, food, water, shelter, sleep

In this chapter, I'll reveal subtle ways to showcase your awesome self to others – especially men – and how to give them a powerful reason to approach you, all without saying a single word. Because if you're like most women, you prefer the man to approach you. But first, you need to give him the signal it's safe to do so.

Results You'll Get From This Chapter

As you start to dial-in to your new state of Magnetic Approachability, expect to enjoy incredible attraction results such as…

★ Feel comfortable and socially confident around anyone

I used to feel so uncomfortable around people, especially large groups. When I first moved from my hometown of Portland, Oregon to the big city of Chicago in 2010, I'd never taken public transportation before. The L train commute during rush hour with hundreds of people jammed into a small space together was a truly terrifying experience.

But after a few months of riding the train twice a day to work and back, I became desensitized and even comfortable with it – to the point where I'd spot two inches of available space on the train and squeeze myself in there, touching six or seven strangers in the process with zero hesitation. This chapter will help you be on your way to the same level of social comfort – without having to brave big-city transit at rush hour.

★ Never feel "invisible" again

If you've ever been passed-up by a man, especially when out with your friends who seem to get all his attention instead, it can feel so defeating.

The approachability techniques in this chapter will help make those days a thing of the past. Your presence will no longer go unnoticed; you'll be the one who stands out from the crowd and silently commands the attention of great men.

★ Inspire him to approach, so you have zero risk of rejection

A man's decision of whether to approach you or not usually boils down to how much risk he thinks it involves. He doesn't know you yet, so engaging you risks rejection or even public humiliation. That's why when you give him the right signals that you're open to engaging, it lowers his perceived risk which can make him more willing to go for it.

Inspiring a man to approach you gives you the luxury of avoiding that gamble yourself; he's assuming 100% of the downside in that moment, so remember that every time a man engages you. On some level he's nervous, but he felt you were worth the risk, so please be kind to him.

Note: You can absolutely approach him too. I'll show you how to overcome the fears associated with that in *Chapter II: Effortless Engagement*.

★ Attract the right man like a magnet (without saying a word)

One of the best parts about these approachability techniques is that none of them require you to say a single word. We'll cover easy ways to break the ice with anyone – including men you're attracted to – in *Chapter II: Effortless Engagement*.

The Irresistible Woman: Authentic, Alluring, and *Approachable*

"A good man doesn't need to break down or scale your wall. He's just going to look for a warm, inviting, open door."

    – Evan Marc Katz, dating and relationship expert

So what exactly does "approachability" mean? Here's my definition…

Approachability is creating a safe space for others to engage with you by removing barriers and lowering their perceived risk of rejection.

When you're truly comfortable with yourself and your surroundings, people are naturally drawn to you. The higher your approachability factor, the more comfortable people will feel around you – and it's all done by sending out just a few subtle, but powerful, signals.

Caution: Powerful magnetic field ahead

"You should think about the consequence of your magnetic field being a little too strong."

    – Taylor Swift, "Gorgeous"

Applying these simple yet powerful approachability tips means you're going to start attracting a lot of people. So make sure you're checking in with yourself and choosing to pursue connections with the ones who add value to your life and make you feel good.

Location is Everything

As an offline dating coach, the number one question I get asked by women is "Where do I go to meet great single men?"

My answer is always the same: **everywhere!**

Think about all the errands you run (coffee shop, bank, dry cleaners), your commute to work (bus, train, carpool, rideshare, walking, parking garage), grabbing your morning latte at the local coffee shop or lunch at your favorite Greek deli, meeting a friend out for dinner, walking your dog around the neighborhood, running a 5K, taking a cooking class, and so much more.

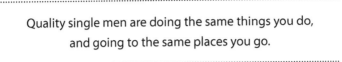

> Quality single men are doing the same things you do,
> and going to the same places you go.

You don't need to go to a bar to meet men; although that can work too. Personally, I prefer meeting men during the day because I'm simply being my authentic self in everyday places, which naturally attracts the right people to me.

Here's a list of places other than bars that I've been asked out – I've put my personal favorites in **bold**:

- Walking down the street
- **Airport and Airplane**
- Grocery store
- Animal shelter
- Greeting card aisle of drug store
- **Charity event**
- Coffee shop
- **House party**
- Bus stop
- Rideshare carpool
- My high school reunion
- Apartment lobby
- **Visiting friends out of town**
- Barbeque picnic
- Train
- **Concert**
- Wedding
- **Birthday party**
- Work

Think of some places you frequent – I'm willing to bet there's an opportunity to meet a guy at most of them. I even met a great man at a child's first birthday party, so you honestly never know.

Also make it a point to go to places where people are gathered to socialize such as hiking groups, wine tastings, volunteering or events posted on sites like Meetup.com and Eventbrite. Most people gather at these events to enjoy the social aspect and meet new people, thus it's easier to chat up a stranger who's there for the same reasons you are.

Note: just because you're in a casual environment doesn't mean you're surrounded by boring people. Even the most interesting and intellectual movers and shakers of the world still need to buy cereal and renew their driver's license. So keep an open mind as you move through seemingly "mundane" places like the grocery store and the DMV. Interesting people can be found in the most offhand of places. Who knows, you might find a gem of guy at the post office!

Simple Social Warm-Ups

Feeling a little shy about meeting men in everyday places? Here are four approaches to ease into a state of Magnetic Approachability:

#1 The Value of Volunteering

A good place to start warming-up your social and approachability skills is by volunteering. You'll have a purpose for being there and be focused on an activity, which allows for natural pauses. Plus, you have a built-in conversation topic! We'll get into icebreakers in *Chapter II: Effortless Engagement*, but here's a preview of questions to ask at a volunteer event:

- *"What's your connection to the cause?"*
- *"How long have you been helping out here?"*
- *"What's your favorite part about coming here?"*

Volunteering can also help you discover a hidden passion or even your life purpose, which will lead to a more fulfilling life. There's also a great chance you'll run into some like-minded men there, who value giving back to the community too. What a sexy trait!

#2 The Vacation Mindset

The Vacation Mindset comes into play whenever you go outside of your normal environment by giving you the chance to experiment in situations where you're unlikely to see the same people again.

Your inhibitions are lowered because your fear of seeing someone you know – and thus your risk of being judged by them – is taken off the table. It's like, "Whatever happens in Vegas stays in Vegas".

The best part is you don't even have to go on vacation to tap into this powerful technique. Simply change-up your daily routine by going to a different movie theater, a different coffee shop, or taking a different bus route home.

While perusing these new places, apply one or two of the approachability tips from this chapter that are just outside of your comfort zone. Because when you're trying them out at that coffee shop across town, telling yourself you never have to go back there can take the pressure off and quell any fears of embarrassment in front of people you'll never have to see again.

#3 Alone = Approachable

"I'm very social, but the thought of getting turned down in front of half the bar terrifies me."
  – Tom, my friend

The majority of my ask-outs have happened when I was by myself. Men can feel intimidated by groups of girls because the risk of rejection swells from potential humiliation by just one person to now many people.

It can feel scary to talk to strangers when you don't know how they'll react, let alone do it in front of others who are watching and potentially judging you as you do it. That's why going places by yourself makes it even safer for a man to approach you.

For example, after flirting with my male gym receptionist for weeks, one night I was the last member to leave. As I passed by his desk, he asked if I'd like to join him at a party later that night and we exchanged numbers. Clearly, he saw that as a great opportunity to finally make his move because no one else was around to judge him if I'd declined.

If you're uncomfortable going places alone, it's completely possible to work your way up to it. Push your limits by stepping out solo to a place that's just outside your comfort zone. The first time you go there alone it may feel awkward – but by the third or fourth time, it will start to feel comfortable. This is how I conquered this fear, which was actually a fear of being judged as a loner with no friends.

I learned another technique from my mom, who grew up with the same fear of being judged for showing up alone. She'd push herself to go to a party alone and meet one new person before she allowed herself to leave. As she became more socially confident, she'd push herself to stay until she met two new people, then three. It wasn't long before she'd conquered her fears and was shutting down the parties!

Just remember: only go alone to places that you feel safe doing so. When in doubt, before you go out, tell a trusted friend where you're headed and what time you'll be back, so there's an extra level of accountability.

#4 The 20-Minute Trick

A great way to get comfortable going places alone is by arriving twenty minutes early for a planned meet-up with other people. Twenty minutes is the perfect window of time to get comfortable being by yourself because you have a real purpose for being there – you just "happened" to arrive a little early.

We tend to think thoughts such as, "I can't go out to dinner by myself, only losers go out to dinner by themselves." Sometimes it stems from a past event – like when you were ten years old riding the school bus and heard the neighborhood bully call little Suzie a loser because she was sitting in a seat by herself. In that seemingly small but significant moment, a seed was planted, associating sitting alone with being judged as a loser, and sprouted a powerful – albeit subconscious – thought that prevented you from going places alone for decades afterward.

Despite what I once believed, there is NOT some official list of activities that are "socially unacceptable" to do alone.

You're not only allowed but *highly encouraged* to do any activity by yourself, which will also help you get comfortable with your own company.

I love going places by myself – like the movies. I can see whatever film I want, at whichever showtime I want, and there's no need to schedule around someone else or feel bad if I drag a friend to what ends up being a dud. One of my clients, Penny, went to a movie by herself and was asked out by a guy who was there by himself too. Bottom line, permission granted to do any and everything alone that you want to as long as you feel safe.

If you think about it, men do things alone all the time. They go to sporting events by themselves. They go to bars by themselves. I've seen guys reading newspapers at brunch by themselves. So if men can do all those things alone, take heart that you as a woman can too.

After you get comfortable being alone for twenty minutes before your friends arrive, next time push it to arriving thirty minutes early, then forty-five minutes. Once you have enough experiences to prove to yourself the fears of going somewhere solo aren't real, you'll be able to go anywhere by yourself sans plans with others, because you've discovered the joy of your own fabulous company.

Action Items

1. Describe how you feel when you're surrounded by strangers.
2. What's your first reaction when a stranger approaches you?
3. What's one place you can be alone for just 20 minutes?

The #1 Principle of Approachability

"When we're driven by speed and mindlessness, we ignore or edit what most of our senses are telling us. We might even overlook the love of our life."
– Susan Gillis Chapman, *The Five Keys of Mindful Communication*

Settling into the present moment allows you to be aware of life happening around you – the sounds, the scents, the people. By practicing being present, everything you learn in this book will amplify your magnetic approachability results ten-fold.

> Being present is the number one way to become a
> magnetically approachable woman.

Being present in the moment is the first key step to creating any type of meaningful connection – from chatting-up a woman behind you at the coffee shop to getting a date with a guy in the cleaning supplies aisle of the drug store. Being present makes you aware of the people around you and creates a safe space for them to take the lead to engage with you.

Question: how present are you in your life? As you go about your day are you mentally running through your "To Do" list or are you tuned-in to your surroundings – such as feeling your shoes snug around your feet, or enjoying that slight whiff of cologne from the man standing next to you at the farmers market as you're picking out cucumbers.

> Put aside thoughts about the past and the future
> so you can experience the *right now*.

Notice the man who stood at the door a few seconds longer so he could hold it open for you – and thank him by making eye contact and flashing a genuine smile. Ask how your waitress's day is going, and truly mean it as you say it.

Being present will also feel like you have more time in your day. Noticing things and people around you increases the number of experiences you remember. The more experiences you remember, the more it can feel like life is slowing down in a great way. Note: this only works for experiences that engage you on a sensory level – i.e. not from behind a screen.

Seven Ways to Snap Into the Present

Here are seven different ways to get out of your head and into the present:

#1 Meditate

The first way is to meditate, and there are plenty of phone apps to help you with that. I do a five-minute meditation every morning, with the goal to eventually expand to ten, then fifteen minutes. Taking just a few minutes every morning to call attention to the here and now sets the stage for heightened sensory experiences throughout the rest of your day.

#2 Capture Your Thoughts

Choose a go-to place to capture your random thoughts and insights as they pop-up. The goal is to get those future "To Do's" out of your head and into a place where you can put them into action later, thus freeing up your mind to be present in the moment without losing the new idea.

For instance, maybe you're at H&M browsing for a dress to wear to your niece's wedding when the thought hits you, "Oh shoot, I forgot to call Dad back – don't forget, call Dad back." You've now shifted your attention to not forgetting a future event and completely pulled yourself away from everything happening around you right now. That means anyone who wants to engage with you will likely sense your distraction and won't feel comfortable disturbing you.

The key is to capture your thoughts in a single place and get into the habit of checking that resource regularly, so you know your ideas are waiting for you at the end of the day when you're ready to revisit them.

My personal go-to capture method is emailing myself because I clean out my inbox at the end of every day. If you're not a crazy Inbox Zero fanatic like I am, try using a notes app (e.g. OneNote and Evernote) or even carry an old-school notepad and pen in your purse.

#3 Notice Your Breath

Humans breathe approximately 23,000 times per day, but most of us give zero attention to it.

Focusing on even just a handful of those breaths will call your attention back to the present moment. Feel your chest rise and fall, and the air moving through your throat. Notice if you're breathing through your nose or your mouth.

#4 Indulge Your Senses

A big part of being present stems from getting out of your head and into your body. A quick way to do that is by relishing anything sensory. Eating is a great example since it's an activity you do several times per day, every day. At your next meal, note the colors of the food on your plate, how they smell, their different textures, and the taste of each bite.

#5 People-Watch

People-watching is a personal favorite pastime of mine that helps me become present. It's always fun to check out your fellow humans and serves as a wonderful reminder that I'm a member of a group, a community, a species – that I'm not alone.

Note the facial expressions and movements of different people as they come into your line of vision. Does that man look confident? Is that woman in a rush? Is that little boy on the verge of a tantrum?

Don't let your thoughts go to a place of judgment, just observe them. If you find yourself going down the judgment road, turn those thoughts into compliments about the person. That will instantly flip that negative script into positivity and appreciation. We'll cover more on how to release judgment about yourself and others in *Chapter III: Asked Out Organically*.

#6 Acknowledge Someone

"I like to think of smiling, eye contact, and flirting as intangible gifts you give to other people. You could have been aloof like others tend to be, but you chose otherwise. So whoever gets your gifts should appreciate them."
　　– Sophia, my client

Another way to snap into presence is to acknowledge other people. That could be as simple as flashing a smile, making eye contact, or putting your hand on someone's back as you brush past them in a tight space.

#7 Paint a Mental Picture

I saved my favorite tip for last because this one's a life-changer. As you're going about your day, notice the noises and images around you and picture who or what is behind them. Heck, go a step further and create your own little story about them. If there's a bird chirping, where is it? What kind of bird is it? What does it look like and what is it chirping at?

The Aston Martin that just sped past you: was it a mid-life crisis purchase, a self-made millionaire, or a local celebrity? Picture in your mind the person behind the wheel and imagine their story. Where are they coming from? Where are they headed? Get creative and have fun with it!

Action Items

1. Choose one of the seven ways to snap into the present and practice it the next time you head out:
   #1 A meditation app
   #2 Have <u>one</u> go-to place to capture your thoughts
   #3 Focus attention on your breath
   #4 Relish anything sensory
   #5 People-watch
   #6 Acknowledge others
   #7 Paint a mental picture
2. Why did you choose that approach over the others?

Three Pillars of Magnetic Approachability

Next up, we'll cover how to master the three pillars of approachability…

1) Prepping
2) Positioning
3) Projecting

The first pillar, Prepping, is all about boosting your social confidence before you leave the house.

The second pillar, Positioning, shows you how to build a habit of social awareness and choose the best spot when you're out and about that maximizes your opportunities for connection.

The last pillar is Projecting, where you'll apply simple tips to subtly exude a state of Magnetic Approachability to everyone around you – without saying a word, of course.

Pillar 1: Prepping

Becoming an open and approachable woman starts before you step foot out your front door. Here are two ways to boost your Magnetic Approachability powers as you're preparing to head out.

#1 Set a Powerful Intention

The first way to become more approachable is a simple but powerful tip: set an intention of your social goal for the day. The intention doesn't always have to be "Get a date," it could be "Get comfortable going to a new place alone" or "Smile at three people while on my run."

My friend and fellow dating coach, Jonathon Aslay, has a sign hanging next to his front door that reads "I am open and receptive to love," which provides a friendly reminder every time he steps outside.

Regardless of what happens after you leave the house, taking a few seconds to set an intention keeps your attention focused on the present moment, which as we covered earlier comes with its own awesome benefits.

Action Items

1. Write down an intention about your social goal for the day.
2. Hold it in your mind throughout your day and watch for opportunities to create that encounter.
3. Describe three positive outcomes that might happen if your intention becomes a reality.

#2 Dress for Confidence + a Conversation

"Clean shirt, new shoes…
Silk suit, black tie…
They come runnin' just as fast as they can
'Cause every girl crazy 'bout a sharp dressed man."
        – ZZ Top, "Sharp Dressed Man"

The next way to prep for approachability is to dress for confidence and a conversation, and I'll give you plenty of different options to choose from with this one.

Whether it's fair or not, people will make instantaneous assumptions about you based on your appearance. As one journalist put it…

"We humans are walking billboards for who we are. Everything about your appearance – height, weight, body language, clothing – conveys data about your socioeconomical background, education level, health, and even grooming habits, all of which are critical fodder for the brain's attraction algorithm."
        – Ginny Graves, "All About Attraction" Time special report magazine
        The Science of Marriage

And one of the best ways to give an impression that you're proud of is by sporting an outfit that makes you feel like a million bucks.

Clothes help you express your personality, interests, values, and passions before you even open your mouth. They also provide an easy and instant conversation starter for men who are dying to talk to you but may not know what to say in the moment.

Plus, let's be honest, people tend to be attracted to others who put a little effort into their appearance. I mean, which man would you feel more drawn to: a guy in a grubby, pit-stained Hanes t-shirt or a man in a crisp, fitted button-down shirt?

As I like to say: change your clothes, change your energy.

The best meeting and dating attire are outfits that are comfortable, make you feel confident, and stand out from the crowd in a unique way. Don't swap comfort for style, like that pair of sexy heels that are strangling your feet with every step. Not only will you be walking as awkwardly as a newborn baby deer by the end of the night, but you won't be able to focus on chatting-up that cute man at the bar because all you can think about are how much you want to be barefoot right now. Instead, swap out those killer shoes for a pair of comfy ballet flats or kitten heels.

Great meeting attire also doesn't remind you of work. There's a feeling of freshness and empowerment when you change-up your wardrobe after work before heading out to a social event or a date. It helps leave the energy of the office behind and starts off your new adventure on a different, much more fun and personal note.

Dress for Confidence

"Enclothed cognition" is a term coined by Dr. Adam Galinsky, a professor at Chicago's Northwestern University, which describes how what you wear affects how you behave. Or as elite athletic coach and author Todd Herman describes it: "putting on stuff that makes you feel like a badass, makes you behave like a badass."

Harness the power of this natural phenomenon and use it to boost your confidence and showcase your personality to become magnetically approachable. Read on for three ways to do it…

i. Boost your confidence

"What one wears on the outside affects how they feel on the inside."
 – Cynthia Rowley, fashion designer

Overall, your clothes tend to either be a confidence booster or a confidence barrier. Wearing an outfit that makes you feel great naturally spreads confidence to other parts of you, such as your posture and conversation skills.

When I taught live workshops, one of the attendees emailed me a few months later to share the great news that she'd found an amazing boyfriend by using my approaches. When I asked which of my tips had been most instrumental in attracting him, she said…

"I focused on putting more effort into my appearance. I was getting lazy unless I was going out for some reason. An additional benefit to focusing on this has been I've felt more confident and happier in general – when you look good, you feel good."

– Vanessa, my workshop student

....

Your external appearance tends to reflect
your internal emotions.

....

As you're planning your day, wear something that feels comfortable but also makes you confident. For example, if you're going to the gym and then to run errands afterward, bring a makeup bag and a change of clothes with you.

ii. Harness the power of another persona

"Your inner hero isn't there to change who you are at your core. It's there to unlock the capability that's always been inside of you."

– Todd Herman, high-performance athletic coach and author

There's a power in leading with a side of yourself that you don't typically show other people. And bringing that secret side to the surface can be as simple as changing up your wardrobe. That way you'll feel fresh and ready to mingle, as opposed to grubby and trying to avoid attention.

Todd Herman shares how he did this with a simple pair of glasses. When he was first starting out as a coach, part of him felt too young and inexperienced to be taken seriously. So he took a fashion cue from Superman and donned a pair of non-prescription glasses, even though he didn't actually need them to see. That prop was the perfect trigger to tap into his confident alter-ego that helped him achieve his goals and – more importantly – feel worthy of them.

Todd   **Alter-Ego Todd**

This alter-ego phenomenon helps sidestep your insecurities and show people a part of you they may not know about. Different clothes, different environments, and different people all bring out different sides of your personality, and it can be fun to explore and showcase that.

Wearing something new or different – even a friend's sweater you borrowed – can lower your inhibition because it makes situations feel less personal. It's like dressing up in a Halloween costume allows you to be a little bolder with your words and actions because you're literally wearing a mask or playing a role that isn't your "real" self, so any reaction from another person isn't taken as personally.

When I first started teaching workshops and was nervous about presenting my new material to people, I wore glasses to give myself an extra feeling of security and bring out my "teaching" persona.

iii. Show respect for yourself and others

"If you look like you care, I'm going to show you that I care."
    – Aaron, my friend and former Chicago Top Single

Putting a little effort into your appearance also shows that you value yourself and care about the impression you're making on other people.

My friend who's a flight attendant said that she's more likely to give freebies to people who are dressed nicely because it shows a respect for themselves and others.

....

You tend to get treated with the same amount of thought and care that you put into your appearance.

....

This phenomenon of being treated according to how you're dressed may not be "fair," but it is what it is. So why not use this to your advantage and work with it, as opposed to fighting an uphill battle against human nature?

Action Items

1. What's one outfit or piece of clothing that makes you feel like a million bucks?
2. Do you wear it only on special occasions? Why or why not?
3. Name one place you've never worn it but would secretly love to – then wear it there!

Dress for a Conversation

"Dress for a party every day and the party will come to you."
  – Steve Edge, branding guru

Men are visual creatures so one of the easiest ways for a man to start a conversation with you is to comment on something you're wearing. Think about it from his perspective: you catch his eye and he has just a few seconds to get your attention before you're on your way and he never sees you again.

Good men can also have a fear of being creepy, so clothes are often a safe topic for them to open a conversation with. So don't be shy with using your clothing as an attraction tool to boost your confidence, help you stand out from the crowd, and give a man an easy way to approach you.

Side Note: we've covered a lot of tips for "How to Dress for Confidence and a Conversation." If it'd be helpful to see a visual of how they all flow together, check out *Guide: All Book Sections by Page Number* on page 237. It's liked a fully extended Table of Contents for the entire book.

i. Make a (silent) personal statement

"Dressing well won't replace qualities like intelligence, kindness, or sense of humor; but it might help communicate those qualities very powerfully."
  – Varvara, my friend

Your clothes are almost always the first impression you give someone – which is great news because you have the power to choose what that impression is. Use your outfits and accessories to express your mood, personality, interests, and/or passions. If you make your own jewelry or have a love of trucker hats, show it off! Then when someone compliments or comments on that piece, the interaction becomes even more personal and kicks off on a topic you love.

Other "personal statement pieces" include piercings, tattoos, a bright nail polish color, or anything that shows off your personality and gives a guy an instant item to comment on.

You can also sport a unique pattern or color. Years ago, I heard someone say "Dudes love red," and I like the power of that simple statement. The color you wear doesn't have to be red, it could be any shade you adore that stands out from the sea of black, white, brown, and grey that most people tend to default to. Try green, blue, yellow, purple, orange, or – my personal favorite – gold.

You want people to see you and instantly wonder "Who's that woman in the bright red coat?" or "What a beautiful green scarf!" You rarely hear anyone say, "Who's that in black?"

ii. Attract like-minded people

Dressing for confidence and a conversation also attracts like-minded people to you. Sporting a bag from your charity of choice or a shirt from a local music festival makes it easy for someone who's into or curious about it to use it as an icebreaker with you.

The more unique the clothing and accessories you wear are, the better. My client Jody is a professor who used to teach in upstate New York before moving to a university in California. One day at her new gym she was wearing her "FLX" shirt, which referred to the Finger Lakes region near her former school. A man came up and asked her about it, and they ended up chatting for twenty minutes. That shirt may have been common back in New York, but it was a rarity in California, so it created the perfect excuse for him to engage her by asking about it.

iii. Get noticed naturally

"What blends in gets forgotten. What stands out gets remembered."
  – Derek Halpern, *How to Find Your Voice - And Own It*

Read on for a few more subtle ways to stand out amongst the masses…

Mismatch your environment

Growing up in Portland, Oregon in the '90s meant I was raised on alternative music; my favorite band is Stone Temple Pilots. Back in those days, I used to go to concerts and, even as a teenager, felt the need to stand out from the crowd – literally.

While twenty-thousand other people were wearing a graphic t-shirt of the band, I would wear cute little lacy tops and dangly earrings (just in case the late great Scott Weiland happened to look my way).

Leave your name tag on

Another subtle way to stand out is to purposefully leave a name tag on after an event. I did this accidentally a few times before I noticed that men kept using it as an excuse to approach me.

After I started purposefully doing it, it was fun to watch the men who thought they were so clever by saying "Hi Camille!" to me, a stranger, and thinking they'd caught me off-guard. Little did they know I was fully aware of what was happening!

Step up + dress up

A person who dresses a step above what everyone else is wearing always stands out from the crowd, especially as society continues to trend toward casual. In my corporate days, sometimes I'd walk around downtown Chicago on my lunch break, wearing my work clothes like a pencil skirt and gold ballet flats; those were a stark contrast to all the tourists sporting ripped jeans and sneakers.

So no need to save your favorite red dress for a "special occasion" – that means you might only wear it, what, twice a year? Throw it on the next time you head to the museum.

Permission granted to dress fancy without an excuse. Before coming to visit me one weekend, my friend Julia sent me this text message and I LOVED her idea…

We hit the town that night in our fancy dresses and had men coming up to us all evening – one even asked to take both of us to dinner.

Action Items

1. What piece of clothing, accessory, or personal feature do you get most complimented on?
2. Why do you think it gets that attention?
3. How can you add more compliment-worthy aspects like that to your everyday look?

Pillar 2: Positioning

Being approachable also means being aware of your surroundings and placing yourself in the right spot. These two simple moves make it easier to casually strike up a conversation with a man who catches your eye. Let's walk through how to do both…

#1 Case the Joint

Every time you step into a new environment (e.g. lobby, train, bus, patio), pause a second and do a quick scan of the place. This move creates the perfect opportunity to show people you've arrived and plant the seed for them to wonder "Hmmm who's that?"

Here are four ways to own a room the second you step into it:

#1 Look around the room as if you're searching for someone specific.

#2 Pretend you're walking into a place you just bought and you're assessing your new digs.

#3 Visualize your energy spreading across the room, out to every corner, and claim the room as yours.

#4 Look at the people in the place and think to yourself "Okay, who gets the awesome experience of talking to me next?"

Doing the scan also gives you the chance to lock eyes with the single men in the room, which helps create that safe space for him to approach you. Again, men have a fear of being creepy which prevents many of them from approaching women they'd otherwise love to engage with. So by locking eyes and creating a split-second mutual acknowledgment of each other, you lower that fear for him.

How do you spot the single men? Simple: they're the ones who tend to be looking around the room. It's in the single man's nature to be constantly surveying and "on the hunt," whether he's consciously aware of it or not. When I'm people-watching, I can usually spot the single men (or ones who wish they were single) in the space based on their reaction – or lack thereof – when an attractive woman enters the scene.

Scanning your new environment also gives you the chance to assess compatibility with men in the room. If a man is dressed in a suit, he likely has a job or is at least interviewing for one. If he's smoking, and that's a deal-breaker for you, you know that up front in case you end up connecting with him later.

Be prepared, not scared

Another benefit of scanning a place upon entry is that it's great for safety and awareness purposes by helping you avoid getting caught off-guard. Or as I like to say, "Be prepared, not scared." It's also been shown that making eye contact with a would-be attacker makes him less likely to target you because he knows you can now identify him.

Use your peripheral powers

A great way to warm-up your scan-abilities and become more socially aware in general is by using your peripheral vision.

You already use your peripheral powers when driving, since you can't focus exclusively on the road ahead of you; you need to be aware of any cars passing you, if the light's about to change, or that car behind you has sirens on top of it. You can use these powers as an approachability tool off the road to become aware of who and what is around you.

An odd example of using my peripheral vision was in line at a café when I noticed out of the corner of my eye the woman behind the cash register made a strange movement. At first, I thought she was drunk. But a few seconds later she had a seizure (she ended up being ok). That strange movement was likely a precursor to it, and I caught it because I was simply aware of my surroundings and knew the way she had moved didn't look normal.

A fun way to hone your peripheral vision is by spotting someone out of the corner of your eye and trying to guess their age and gender by the way they're moving, without looking directly at them. Make your guess, then turn to look directly at them and see if you're correct.

#2 Scout Your Spot

When you have the option of a few different spots (like seats at a bar, or on a bus, or in a lobby), take a moment to select a good one. After doing the scan and noticing a man seated alone who looks interesting, choose the spot a few seats away from him so you're within earshot of each other; or heck, sit down next to him! Don't expect a man to walk across the room and approach you, because odds are most men are too terrified to do that. I certainly would be.

> Making it easy for a man to engage you can be as simple as putting yourself within close proximity of him.

Choosing the right spot can be the difference between meeting an amazing person you spend the rest of your life with and meeting absolutely no one. So take an extra second to choose wisely.

To feel comfortable in the moment of scouting your spot, just pretend like you're looking for someone, so you don't feel pressured to just choose any. If you grab the first seat available with zero thought it may be too late when you notice there's an empty chair next to a cute guy who's sitting alone.

For example, one night I was meeting a few girlfriends at an Italian restaurant for dinner and – taking my own advice – I arrived twenty minutes early to see if I could meet someone new. When I walked into the bar I did a quick scan and saw there were only two spots available: one was just a few feet away next to a man and a woman who were totally absorbed in each other; the other was at the opposite end of the bar between two men who were both clearly there by themselves. Which one do you think I chose? The one in between the men, duh.

I sat down, ordered a glass of wine, kept my phone in my purse (another key approachability tip), and enjoyed a quiet moment to myself. Sure enough, within a few seconds, the man on my right started talking to me, using the topic of construction at the park across the street as his icebreaker.

⫙ Pillar 3: Projecting

Now that you're looking good, feeling good, and know how to grab a great spot in any location, I'll show you how to send the right signals out. Below are seven ways to help you ooze approachability so you can attract a great man like a magnet.

#1 Keep a Headphone Out

"That Walkman; it makes you very unapproachable!"
– Guidance counselor to Rory Gilmore, *Gilmore Girls*

I love listening to my favorite Pandora station while out and about and adding a soundtrack to my surroundings. But headphones can also create an engagement barrier, so skip them once in a while or keep one out of your ear to see what serendipitous opportunities start opening up.

#2 Body Language Basics

When you feel comfortable and relaxed, it naturally makes the people around you feel comfortable, which means they're more likely to approach you.

If you're holding tension in your shoulders after an intense workout or getting annoyed at that loud group of teenagers that just walked onto the subway, other people will sense your uneasiness.

General rule of body language:
if you *feel* uncomfortable, you *look* uncomfortable.

Most people aren't consciously thinking "That woman looks unapproachable;" they just don't feel safe engaging someone who is clearly not at ease with themselves or the situation.

For visual examples of this phenomenon, go to any stock photo website (e.g. Shutterstock, iStock Photo) and search on the term "couples in love." You'll see about three out of every five pictures are two people who are doing something no real couple would ever do (e.g. forming a heart with their hands for the camera or having a picnic in the middle of the road) or clearly forcing a moment by pretending to like each other even though their body language and facial expressions say the opposite. Some of the really awkward ones will make you feel uncomfortable just looking at them.

Now that you know the importance of being comfortable in any environment, here are four ways to instantly shift into approachable body language…

i. Imaginary Party Trick

No matter where you are and who you're surrounded by, pretend like you're hosting a party in your home for your closest friends. Imagine you personally invited every stranger around you, which will help you drop your guard, ease into the moment, and feel the same relaxed state you do when you're at home. In *Chapter II: Effortless Engagement* I'll show you how to use this same concept to confidently start a conversation with a stranger.

ii. Mental body scan

Close your eyes and mentally scan your body to locate where you might be holding any tension. Start with your feet, then slowly move up to your ankles, to your calves, your knees and beyond, intentionally relaxing each part as you go. You may not know that you have an instinctive need to protect your neck (there are some vital arteries in there) and that subconscious reflex can easily lead to tension and tightness in that area in an effort to guard it. If you feel yourself tensing up, take a deep breath, relax your shoulders, and comfortably settle into your position with a little shimmy.

iii. Open yourself up to the world

If you're seated, go a step further from relaxing your muscles by spreading your arms out on both sides away from your body and physically opening yourself up. Taking up space in this way also makes you look and feel extremely confident.

I used this "open up" technique to get asked out by a man on a train ride home one night – ironically after teaching a dating workshop called MANifesting. The train was almost empty, so when I saw a cute guy get on and sit a few seats over from me, with no one in between us, I draped my left arm out over the back of the seat next to me, in his direction, to give off an "I'm open to engaging" vibe.

Sure enough, he got the cue and a few seconds later he leaned over to say, "I like your jacket," and we started chatting. Unfortunately, he completely missed the *other* cues that my stop was coming up, even when I got up and stood by the exit door. So as the doors opened and I slowly started leaving, he was completely caught off-guard and quickly *yelled* his email address to me so we could continue our conversation. Luckily, I have a good memory and was able to quickly write it down.

iv. Secretly synchronize

Another way to catch the attention of someone is to mirror their body language and/or purposefully position yourself toward them. For instance, if a man is sitting next to you in a waiting room, cross your legs toward him. If he's sitting across from you on the bus, hold yourself in a similar stance as his, such as an arm draped across your body in the same way. Obviously don't mimic *everything* he does (creepy!) but observe how he's moving and then put your own spin on it as a subtle way to get his attention and make him feel comfortable – even if he doesn't know why.

#3 Flash a Sexy Glance

"Four minutes of eye contact brings people closer to each other better than everything else."
      – Dr. Arthur Aron[17]

Eye contact can create an instantly intimate moment. There's just something about looking in another person's eyes sharing the experience of being fully seen by them which is so incredibly sexy.

As mentioned in the Introduction of this book, a study done by social scientist Dr. Arthur Aron discovered a scientific approach to help two people fall in love almost instantly. And a key piece of that study was having each pair staring into each other's eyes for four minutes without saying anything.

I did the four-minute stare experiment at a conference with my friend Caitlin V. We were both comfortable with eye contact, and with each other, so we actually enjoyed it once we settled into it.

17 Aron et al., "The Experimental Generation of Interpersonal Closeness: A Procedure and Some Preliminary Findings"

Don't worry, there's no need to master the four-minute stare in order to use eye contact as an attraction tool. I remember from my shy days that even a split-second of meeting someone's gaze can feel very scary. Especially if it's a man you're attracted to.

But after practicing over the years, I've now become almost *too* comfortable with eye contact and need to remember to break my gaze once in a while so I don't creep out the person I'm focused on.

How did I get to that point? I found fun ways to practice and get comfortable with it. Here are my top six ways to master the art of alluring eye contact with anyone…

i. Check out the space

As you're talking to someone look at the space *between* their eyebrows – they won't be able to tell you're looking there, and you won't feel the intensity of directly locking eyes. It's similar to the technique some public speakers use of looking at the top of the heads of people in the audience as opposed to in their eyes, which allows them to come across as engaging without having to be distracted by direct eye contact.

ii. Have a virtual staring contest

Search online for an image of your celebrity crush looking directly at the camera and practice staring back at them for a few minutes each day. Research studies have shown locking eyes with a picture has the same effect on your brain as looking into someone's eyes in person, minus the real-time pressure. After getting comfy staring into Idris Elba's eyes for that long, confidently meeting the gaze of your cute personal trainer will feel like a breeze.

This approach also works with pictures of people in magazines, books, newspapers, and even billboards with pictures of people looking directly out at you. So, permission to make some new two-dimensional friends.

iii. Note his eye color

As you're talking to people throughout your day, make a point to note their eye color. This gives you a reason to look into their eyes a little bit deeper and longer, so you gradually become more and more comfortable with it.

iv. "Looking for someone?"

If you need an excuse to catch the eye of a handsome stranger, look around as if you're searching for a certain person or specific place – like an address. This gives a man the perfect excuse to come up to you and ask, "Are you looking for someone?"

v. Challenge your limit

Continue to push your eye contact comfort zone by holding people's gaze just slightly longer than you're comfortable with, even if it's only an extra half-second. Just like any skill, with a little practice, you too can master the alluring art of eye contact and become too good at it like I am now.

vi. Practice in groups

If you're in a group, look around at each person as you speak to make everyone feel included in the conversation. This is also great for practicing because you're not looking at any one person for more than just a few seconds.

I'll never forget a small group dinner I attended with a man I was dating because he didn't do this, and it made for one incredibly awkward meal. There were only three of us sitting around the table, but every time he spoke, he just stared at our mutual friend, never even giving me a glance. It felt like I was watching their conversation and not actually part of it. So, don't do that. Instead, move your eye contact from one person to the next as you speak and make each person feel like they're equally included.

#4 Prevent "Resting Bitch Face" (in one quick move)

"If you have good thoughts, they will shine out of your face like sunbeams, and you will always look lovely."
    – Roald Dahl, *The Twits*

Smiling is one of the best moves to instantly show someone you're a friendly person who's open to engaging. Smiling paired with eye contact is even more powerful.

Plus, smiling actually puts you in a better mood. By engaging your mouth muscles that form a smile, it triggers "muscle memory" and causes you to feel the same emotions associated with a natural, unplanned smile. Try these two techniques to master the flash of your pearly whites…

i. The Secret Smile

The Secret Smile is any smile that comes from your inner confidence or knowing – like "Oh, wouldn't you like to know what I'm so smiley about?" The secret you're smiling about could simply be that you're doing The Secret Smile.

Think of something that makes you happy, such as a great catch-up session with a friend or getting a text from a guy you like. Channel that joy and gratitude into a nice, big, genuine smile for all to see.

ii. Become a Mouth Breather

If you're not feeling smiley, try breathing through your mouth. This is the instant antidote to "Resting Bitch Face." It's just opening up your mouth a little bit, which sounds small – and weird – but it works incredibly well. Here's a Facebook message my friend, a YouTube star, sent me after practicing the mouth-breathing technique…

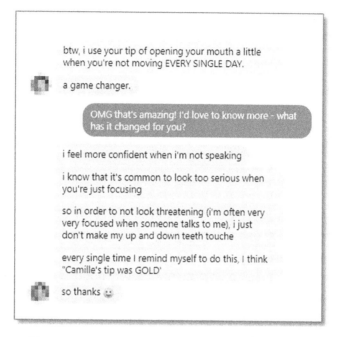

The goal is to create a tiny space by opening your lips, which relaxes your jaw, softens up your facial features, and makes you look open and welcoming. The next time you're in line at the grocery store look at the women on magazine covers; they're almost always smiling or at least have their lips slightly parted as if they're breathing through their mouth.

#5 Start "Squinching"

"The #1 tip I have in my arsenal to make people look more photogenic is squinching. If you're a human who just wants to look hot, better, or more confident... this is gonna do it for you."

— Peter Hurley, celebrity photographer

"Squinching" is a term coined by professional photographer, Peter Hurley. But the benefits go well beyond taking a confident, sexy picture – you can use it to flash a confident, sexy glance to an attractive stranger too.

Squinching = **Squinting** (top eyelids) + **Pinching** (lower eyelids)

The secret to doing the squinch is narrowing the distance between your lower eyelid and your pupil while bringing the top lid down just a tiny bit. The lower eyelid is the same fold of skin that naturally rises up when you're flashing a genuine smile.

Just like with mouth-breathing, most celebrities do some form of squinch for photo ops. Practice your squinch in front of the mirror until you feel like you're starting to nail it and then see what a difference it makes. It's like thinking of something that makes you happy and having that joy come through in your eyes, but being purposeful about it.

Not Squinching   **Squinching**

#6 Be Purposefully Playful

"Humans love play. We learn by play. Locked in our grown-up clothes and calcified social identities, we freakin' YEARN to play."
   – Adam Gilad, dating and relationship expert

When you're in a playful mood, it invites other people to be playful back and create a little moment together. So tap into your fun side around strangers, who are really just friends (or boyfriends) you haven't met yet.

Try moving to the beat of your headphone music while sitting on the bus or singing out loud to the song that's playing in your taxi or rideshare. You can also pick up on subtle or unintentional playful invitations from others. For instance, I was walking down the sidewalk one day and saw two women walking toward me. As we passed each other the older one sang out, "Just a touch... of love..." and without hesitating I chimed in "...a little bit!" because – hey – I like that Keith Sweat song too.

The younger woman smiled back at me and said, "Oh Mom, she's singing with you!" Start showing strangers your playful side, even ones you may not be romantically interested in. Then work your way up to doing it with a man who catches your eye.

#7 Let Him Do It

The last approachability tip is to *let him do it* – with "it" being anything. Men love helping out and doing things for women, even small actions like opening the door, holding the elevator, or getting something off a shelf. It makes them feel needed and useful. They know you can do these things yourself, but they want to do it *for you*. So when a man offers to help you, unless you're getting a seriously creepy vibe from him, let him be the man he wants to be for you in that moment.

Action Items

1. Choose one of the seven ways to project approachability:
   #1 Headphones out
   #2 Body language
   #3 Eye contact
   #4 Smiling
   #5 Squinching
   #6 Be purposefully playful
   #7 Let him do it
2. What's a positive outcome that might come from applying it?

And those were the three Pillars of Approachability, congratulations for making it through Chapter I!

Coming Up Next...

In the next section *Chapter II: Effortless Engagement*, I'll show you how to easily chat-up all the people who are being magnetically drawn to you, as well as discover...

- How to stop conversations from draining the life out of you
- How to break out of shyness and gain conversation confidence
- Eleven scripts to break the ice with anyone
- How to make every icebreaker feel natural
- Four easy ways to never forget someone's name again
- How to validate yourself by simply talking to strangers
- How to know exactly what to say when he approaches you
- How to never feel the pain of a missed opportunity ever again
- How to transition off the icebreaker and into a conversation
- The quickest (and kindest) scripts to get out of any conversation

CHAPTER II

Effortless Engagement

*Discover how to talk to any
man with zero risk of rejection
(even if you're shy)*

Once you know my secret to start a conversation with anyone, a whole new world of amazing men will be revealed to you.

In this section we're building upon the social comfort you gained in *Chapter I: Magnetic Approachability* to create confidence in your conversation skills. In terms of Maslow, now that you know how to meet your need for Safety and Security in Chapter I, you can move to the next level of Love and Belonging in Chapter II.

Maslow's Hierarchy of Needs

Self-Actualization
morality, problem solving, creativity, lack of prejudice

Self-Esteem
self-confidence, respect of others

Love and Belonging
friendship, family, intimacy, sense of connection

Safety and Security
security of body, employment, resources, health, property

Physiological
air, food, water, shelter, sleep

I'll show you the simple trick to start a conversation with anyone, and how to respond when someone starts one with you. No need to walk up to the hottest guy in the room just yet (although if you feel empowered to do so, awesome!). The techniques you'll discover in this chapter should be applied to everyone you meet – from your favorite female barista to your potential future boyfriend.

Having the power and confidence to talk to anyone is a total life-changer. It means you're just one sentence away from connecting with someone who you could end up sharing your life with. So why isn't everyone taking advantage of all the daily opportunities to chat-up others in the real world??

Two words...

Emotional Labor (it's a thing)

"Emotional labor is the exertion of energy for the purpose of addressing people's feelings, making people comfortable, or living up to social expectations."

> – Suzannah Weiss, "50 Ways People Expect Constant Emotional Labor from Women and Femmes"

Sociologist Arlie Hochschild originally coined the term "emotional labor" in reference to managing expressions and feelings in a job environment – such as a waitress or receptionist always maintaining a pleasant attitude as they serve customers, regardless of how they truly feel.

The definition has since expanded beyond work, now encompassing a woman's tendency to constantly "manage" herself, her feelings, and her interactions with others. Regardless of whether it's a conscious or unconscious effort, the intention behind this arduous process usually stems from a desire to live up to other people's expectations or to be liked by them. And it can feel exhausting.

> Emotional labor is the energy required to maintain
> the gap between your real self and
> the version you're projecting to the world.

Think about it: if you're like most women, you're constantly considering and managing the details of not only your own life but everyone else's life as well.

Here are a few examples...

- *"Manager seems grumpy this morning, better be extra nice so I don't set him off."*
- *"Time to put on a 'happy face' for this client that drives me nuts, so I can keep the relationship intact."*
- *"Did that guy just smile at me? Better smile back so he doesn't think I'm a rude person."*

So what does emotional labor have to do with meeting a great man in the real world?

Everything.

This constant surveillance of your emotions, thoughts, words, and actions requires a ton of energy to maintain. It can also suck the fun out of any conversation and lead you to believe that you "hate talking to people" – despite the fact you can easily chat with your BFF for three-plus hours at a time.

The "draining" aspect of talking to other people comes into play the moment you become more focused on how someone is perceiving you rather than how much you're enjoying the interaction. This often manifests in the form of presenting a more "polished persona" of yourself to the world.

Now, I'm all in favor of making a great first impression – but not at the expense of your happiness, and certainly not in a way that requires you to be anyone other than your authentic self.

Note: if you feel like you're not adopting a different persona in public yet still feel drained by conversations with strangers, you're probably getting stuck in the "Small Talk Trap." In *Chapter III: Asked Out Organically,* you'll learn my secret five-step method to create a meaningful connection with everyone you meet.

Also, with technology providing us with endless entertainment and "connection" options, many people are now out of practice with how to actually *talk* to each other – as in, a face-to-face conversation.

Social skills are like muscles: you're either regularly
strengthening them or actively losing them.

For example, if you haven't chatted-up a stranger in years, you'll likely have some major fear around doing so because it's become unfamiliar territory for you. On the other hand, if you complimented a random woman's hat yesterday, you won't have that same trepidation because you created a recent experience that proved there's nothing to be afraid of.

Even as a social skills coach, I often hole-up for several days to get into deep creative focus on a project. Once I finally re-emerge in the real world, I've noticed it takes a few conversations before I'm fully at ease talking to people again, because even after a few days I'm a little out of practice.

With many people feeling like they have to present a different version of their real self and/or are completely out of conversational practice, it's no wonder people don't talk to each other!

So what's the solution?

Find your flow

"We're drawn to authenticity because it's real and feels good. We all want to live as our most authentic selves 24/7/365, but not everyone has that courage. So if someone is radiating that feeling, we can't help but move towards joining their bubble."
    – Sorinne Ardeleanu, author

What if, instead of feeling like you were "going into battle" every time you had to talk to a new person, you instead felt like you were laying on an innertube, head titled back gazing at the blue sky, floating down a tranquil river to a dreamy destination?

Well, when you find your natural flow with engaging people, you'll be able to enjoy a metaphorically similar experience. Minus the innertube and tranquil river.

So what's the secret to talking to anyone with ease? It's being the same authentic version of yourself with everyone you meet: friends, coworkers, men you're interested in, the check-out clerk, everyone.

Being your same self across every interaction prevents you from expending precious energy trying to keep up whatever alter-persona you've been presenting to the world. It also keeps you energetically aligned and naturally attracts the right people to you – including the right man.

> Every relationship starts with one conversation, so be your real self from the very first word to attract the right people.

Results You'll Get From This Chapter

In this chapter I'll show you how to break free from any emotional labor you've been harboring, so you can enjoy these results in your own life...

★ Never regret another missed opportunity

Back in my super-shy days, it was depressing to watch all my classmates easily connect with each other while I sat there feeling powerless about how to do it myself. If someone tried to talk to me, I never knew how to comfortably handle it, and would simply shut down.

I still cringe at a memory from when I was a fifteen-year-old assistant camp counselor at a state park in Oregon. One of the head counselors, Jason, whom I'd had a crush on all summer, came up and started talking to me. I was so flustered all I could think to do was to pretend to be focused on the clipboard of papers I was holding, giving him short answers, and not even looking him in the eye. After thirty seconds of unsuccessfully trying to engage me, he finally walked away. I felt awful knowing I'd missed out on the opportunity to connect with him, but I'd had no clue how to do it.

★ Errands and chores become romantic adventures

"I used to hate running errands, going to the gym, going to the library, etc. – but now I see them as opportunities to put my cell away, look my best, and be feminine. Having the skills to start conversations with total strangers is invaluable, especially in the technical times we live in. Offline Living Rocks!"
– Shannon, my client

When you have the power to easily talk to anyone, the world becomes less lonely and an everyday errand can become an amazing adventure. You'll see that you're just one sentence away from connecting with anyone you want to – and every conversation you create holds the potential to bring someone new and exciting into your life.

★ Easily talk to anyone (with zero risk of rejection)

Fear of rejection tends to surface when we get too attached to a specific outcome. When you master the art of effortless engagement you focus on the opportunity instead of the outcome – which means there's nothing that can be rejected or disappointing. You're simply the person who casually talks to everyone about everyday topics, focusing more on enjoying the connection rather than achieving a certain goal with it.

Using my approach, your initial investment in an interaction will be so small that even if the other person chooses not to respond, you won't care. Would you feel rejected if you asked the person making your sandwich at Subway for extra pickles and she looked a little annoyed as she added them? Of course not. You'd be happy you got more of your favorite topping and her tiny reaction would never cross your mind again.

★ Feel in complete control of every conversation

Knowing how to talk to anyone doesn't mean you need to talk to *everyone*. It means you have the power to talk to anyone you want, when you want to. You'll no longer be at the mercy of whatever someone else wants to talk about or feeling trapped in an endless and boring conversation. You'll feel more empowered to start a conversation once you know how to make it enjoyable for you and how to gracefully end it any time you want to.

★ Create instant rapport with anyone – from the first word

When you talk to a stranger the same way you talk to a close friend, something magical happens. The person will likely respond to you the same way they would to a friend. Sharing something that's relevant in the moment and in the same casual tone as a friend would say reminds them of other people they know, like, and trust, so they instantly begin to feel the same familiar comfort with you.

This "instant trust" phenomenon isn't usually a conscious one, ("Wow, this random woman is talking to me just like my best friend Ellie does! I'm going to trust her as much as I trust Ellie…") it's usually a feeling that they aren't even aware of ("This person makes me feel comfortable").

People can usually tell when you're being inauthentic or have an ulterior motive (like bragging or selling something), and that tends to keep them stuck on small talk because it feels safer. No one wants to be vulnerable with someone who seems untrustworthy. I'm sure you've experienced this in a conversation with someone where you felt something disingenuous about them. Even if it didn't feel malicious, it probably prevented you from going past basic pleasantries.

★ Naturally attract the right people who adore the real you

"Once you figure out what your voice is, you're in a league of your own, because no one can compete with you being you."
– Matthew Hussey, dating and relationship expert

People can feel it in their bones when a person is being authentic, which means showing your true self to everyone is a powerful way to attract the right people into your life.

> Being your authentic self attracts the right people – including the right man – to you like a magnet.

On the flip side, if you're displaying a fake persona that doesn't show your true self, how are the right people – including your future guy – supposed to find you? What's worse, being anyone other than your real self will start attracting the wrong people to you; the ones who resonate with the phony signal you're emitting. Then when the *real* you appears – which it always does – they'll feel duped at the difference.

I'm acutely aware of this character "bait and switch" because I did it myself for over a decade, especially with men. I used to feel like my real self wasn't interesting or worthy of people I liked, so I'd pretend to be someone I thought the other person was more willing to accept. But as time went on the "real me" started to come out – and suddenly the "play it cool and casual Camille" they'd been initially attracted to was replaced by "insecure Camille who needs a lot of attention."

So if you want to attract the right people – including men – into your life who love and accept the real you, it's your responsibility to show them who you truly are from the very first conversation.

★ Honor your own feelings first

Being your consistent self *doesn't* mean maintaining the same emotional state all day, every day.

For instance, maybe you had a bad morning. You woke up late for work, spilled coffee on your new shirt, and the first email you opened was an annoying request from a high-maintenance client. If you were meeting your best friend for lunch later that day, would you "put on your happy face" for her after a morning like that? Of course not. You'd let her know today ain't the best day ever and you're a little grumpy. You know she loves and accepts you regardless of your mood, and being true to your emotions in that moment feels better than pretending that everything is "just fine, thanks." So honor yourself and how you feel in a similar way with everyone else you encounter too. Pretending to appear any way other than how you truly feel will only make you feel worse.

If you find yourself in a bad mood, obviously don't be rude to people, but maybe give yourself a break from actively engaging with others, or keep interactions to the bare minimum, until it passes. You're always allowed to feel how you feel, and those moods always pass in time.

★ Satisfy your innate need for social connection

"Next to physical survival, the greatest need of a human being is psychological survival: to be understood, to be affirmed, to be validated, and to be appreciated."

– Dr. Stephen Covey, author and thought leader

Engaging with another human fulfills your intrinsic need for social connection, no matter how random or brief the encounter might be. That's why when a person says something random to you, it's usually more about their need for connection than it is about the actual topic. This phenomenon is called a "bid to connect," a term coined by Dr. John Gottman of The Gottman Institute social research organization.

For example, if you're at a coffee shop waiting for your drink order to come up and an elderly woman standing next to you says to you…

"Their bacon quiche here is delicious, have you had it?"

That comment isn't really about the quiche. It's about the woman's need for connection in that moment. So don't get hung up on the topic, just roll with it and share the moment with her by saying something like…

"I haven't tried it, what makes it so yummy?"

It's a simple opportunity for both of you to exchange a few words before you go your separate ways. Plus, you never know where that interaction may lead. Maybe a few seconds later her extremely handsome, single grandson walks up to you two and introduces himself.

★ Validate yourself on a deeper level

"When I was walking down the aisle, I was walking toward somebody who didn't have any idea who I really was. And it was only half the other person's fault, because I had done everything to convince him that I was exactly what he wanted."

– Maggie Carpenter, *Runaway Bride*

If you've been adopting a "polished persona" for a while, you may feel out of touch with how to be your authentic self around others – or worse, convinced yourself that no one would accept the real you. Yet you haven't even given them a chance to. You made that decision for them without even giving them the option to decide for themselves, which has essentially robbed them of the experience of the real you.

That's why a deeper benefit of showing everyone your genuine self is that it validates to *yourself* that the real you is fabulous and worthy of engaging others. Using the techniques in this chapter to achieve that realization will feel incredibly freeing. It will also create a new truth for yourself that overrides any feelings of inadequacy you've developed by limiting how you show up in social situations.

Consistency 101: Your Shift into Effortless Engagement

The habit of showcasing an *inauthentic* alter-ego comes in many forms. These may include, but are not limited to, tailoring yourself to different people and different situations, over-rehearsing what to say in a conversation, and/or just feeling like you need to be "on" in order to interact with people.

Each of those aspects requires energy from you to bridge the gap between the real you and the version you're presenting to the world – so if you've done any of those in the past, it's no wonder you feel drained by social interactions.

In my corporate days when I was attending business networking events, I noticed a lot of women there had an unnaturally high-pitched, fake-feeling voices when they introduced themselves – like…

> *"Hiiiiiiii!! Oh my gosh, it's SO nice to meet you! I LOVE your coat, it's SOOOOOOO pretty!"*

It made me uncomfortable because I felt obligated to match that crazy-high level of energy and enthusiasm, which wasn't how I truly felt. Turns out that's not how they felt or naturally spoke either; they were presenting their hyped-up "networking persona." That meant I had no idea who they truly were and made it impossible to genuinely connect with them.

So if projecting a different persona across every interaction is such a draining process, why do people do it?

Here's Why We're Inconsistent

"Relationships shouldn't be about suckering people in with some sanitized version of yourself, only to spring the real you on them later."
– Rachel Fields, "The Five Stages of Ghosting Grief"

If you feel like you might have a case of the inconsistencies, don't worry; you're not alone. To shine a light on this and start shifting toward more authentic interactions, below are three of the most common reasons people tend to adopt a fake persona and/or fall into energy-draining emotional labor habits.

The first reason is that it can feel safer because if that tone or persona gets "rejected" by someone, it feels less personal. It enables you to tell yourself, "Well, that wasn't the real me anyway!"

The second reason behind the need to "be on" is the desire to create a good first impression with others. Humans have an innate need to be liked and accepted, so after rehearsing a certain "first impression persona" over and over for years, you know the general response it will elicit from others – which likely *isn't* a very deep or meaningful one, but *is* familiar and safe.

The last reason someone may be showcasing a disingenuous version of themselves is simply because it's become a bad habit – something they started doing a long time ago, for whatever reason, and simply never stopped doing it.

Maybe you subconsciously modeled it after a parent or grandparent from an older generation when women were encouraged to always present a sweet and perky version of themselves, regardless of how they truly felt in the moment. And now, every time you walk into a room full of strangers you automatically turn on that "sweet and perky" persona without even realizing it.

It doesn't matter why you adopted a different persona,
only that you stop – and start showing people the real you.

The Instant Cure for Inconsistency

"There are no strangers here; only friends you haven't met yet."
  – William Butler Yeats, Irish poet

So, how do you talk to everyone with ease and show them the real you? Stop distinguishing friends from strangers and talk to everyone the exact same way.

> The key to being your authentic self is to talk to every person you meet as if they're *already* your friend.

Being your consistent self means you have the same mode of (conversation) operation with everyone. That's it. So simple, yet a total social and dating game-changer once you start applying it with everyone – whether you've known them for twenty years or twenty seconds.

When you can relax into every moment and simply be the same person around everyone, you have the power to initiate any interaction, respond to anyone who says something to you, build an instant rapport, and feel totally aligned in the process. The topics of discussion will vary from person to person, but your natural tone and casual style will not.

> Aligning your thoughts and feelings with your words and actions puts you into a state of effortless flow and enjoyment.

The Ellen Effect

"We want to grow, we want to feel good about ourselves, we want to feel proud of who we are. We're all the same. And we are all relatable."
     – Ellen DeGeneres, *Relatable*

To find a model citizen of practicing consistency, look no further than Ellen DeGeneres. Watch any of her videos, from any show, any year – whether it's her 1986 appearance on Johnny Carson (YouTube it) to her 2018 Netflix stand-up special *Relatable*.

You'll see she is the exact same person. Every. Single. Time. This is what I call "The Ellen Effect," and it will transform your interactions when you authentically apply it in your own life.

From the three-year-old who memorized the periodic table of elements to George Clooney, no matter who she's sitting down with on her talk show, Ellen talks to each of them the same way.

Her tone even stays consistent from the very first word – there's no overly-hyped up, high-pitched, "Hiiiiiiiii! I'm so glad you're heeeeeeeeeere!!" like many other hosts default to when introducing a new guest.

Being consistent like this helps people feel like they know her personally and can trust her because you know she will treat you the same way she treats everyone else. Be consistent across all your interactions like Ellen is with hers, and you will never feel drained from social interactions ever again.

But "Consistency" is NOT This...

Note: When I say "be consistent," that does *not* mean to behave the same way all the time. As a human, you experience thousands of thoughts and emotions throughout your day and you should honor each of them as they come up.

....

Alignment is fluid, just like your mood, so stay the course
by being true to your ever-changing self.

....

"Consistency" simply means that your outer actions match your inner feelings in the moment; that the persona you're projecting to the world is a direct reflection of who you truly are – even on your not-so-great days, which everyone has. Forcing your external self to be the opposite of how you're feeling internally is actually what's *inconsistent*.

Of course, there are always situations where we need to adhere to social graces even when it doesn't exactly match how we feel – like having a professional manner at work. But if you find yourself *always* adopting a different persona whenever you're around people, it's time to remedy that exhausting habit.

Take a look at the graphs below for a visual depiction of aligning your emotions with your words and actions ("consistency") versus forcing yourself to act differently than how you actually feel ("inconsistency")...

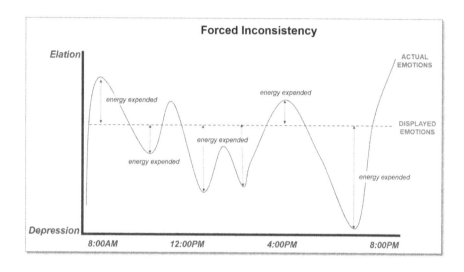

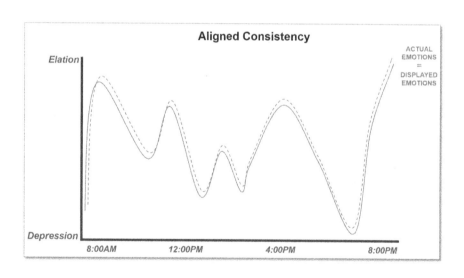

Action Items

1. Do you switch into a different persona depending on which person you're talking to?
2. If so, give an example of what that switch looks like.
3. When did you start adopting that persona?
4. Why do you think you make that switch?
5. Describe how it makes you feel to continually do that.

Two Aspects of Consistency

There are two key aspects to showcasing your consistent self: your script and your tone.

#1 The Script is the Same

Being your consistent self means talking to people about the same random yet relatable topics you'd casually mention to a friend. This approach is especially helpful in breaking the ice with a stranger or when responding to someone who engages you.

To apply it, share with strangers the same random thoughts that pop into your head that you would naturally turn and share with a friend sitting next to you. This is much more natural (and fun!) than putting pressure on yourself to come up with "the perfect line" or over-thinking what you should say. It's a small shift that will take you down a completely different path to an easier and more enjoyable conversation.

Start every new conversation on a casual topic that's instantly relatable to anyone in the moment.

Years ago, in one of my live workshops, I came to this part of the training and one of my attendees, a beautiful black woman in her late twenties, said to me...

"Camille, will you please tell white guys the script is the same? They don't need to come up to me and start talking about Kanye."
    – Cambria, my workshop student

She described how a white guy had tried to engage her using an icebreaker about Kanye West, apparently in an attempt to better relate to her because she was black. But Kanye had nothing to do with anything in that moment, so it totally confused her. Lesson learned: Don't customize what you say to someone based on what you think they want to hear or go overboard in trying to speak to their specific age, race, ethnicity, or any other factor.

Just like most celebrities want to be treated like a normal person, most people want to be seen and spoken to as a fellow human being – not an impersonal demographic. We'll do a deep dive on icebreakers, including the ones that have given me the best results, later in this chapter. But for now, as a general rule, remember that "the script is the same."

Assume everyone gets your awesome sense of humor

"Laughter is the shortest distance between two people."
    – Victor Borge, Danish comedian

Sticking to the same script includes sharing your style of humor with everyone. Maybe you make a funny quip out loud asking what that giant orb in the sky is after such a long dark winter and four out of the five people around don't get the joke. But that one person who does get it will think you're hilarious. And *that* is the person you want to connect with.

Purposefully showcasing your authentic self – especially your humor – is how you find your people, including the right man. I cannot emphasize this enough. It's like casting a fishing line into a huge lake and waiting to see who bites. Adopt a mantra that you say every time you walk into a new space, like "I'm here to share my awesome self – which of you lucky devils is going to get it?" Just make sure the side you're showing is a nice side of your humor and not self-deprecating or judgmental.

Boldly share your quirky sense of humor and
assume everyone gets it – because the right people will.

Here's an example: I was in a restaurant lobby waiting for a friend, watching the rain out the window, when a man walked in and shook off his umbrella. He said to the hostess, "It's pouring, I almost slipped in ten different puddles." Without missing a beat, I said with a smile, "Well don't make it eleven…" and pointed to all the water that had gathered at his feet from his umbrella.

He looked down, laughed, and we started talking. A minute or so later, I received a text from my friend canceling our dinner date, so the man invited me to join him for dinner.

The fact that I shared that comment which showcased my slightly sarcastic sense of humor was a risk. He could have stared at me like I had three heads or become offended. But I took the risk because 1) I thought it was funny and I love to crack myself up, and 2) I didn't need him to validate my awesome sense of humor. So I went for it and ended up attracting a dinner date!

Not everyone is going to get your jokes because not everyone is meant to come into your life. That's another benefit of showcasing your authentic self: it speeds up the filtration process of finding the people you truly resonate with.

An example of this that didn't work out so well was when a client of mine, Harriet, was on the phone with a man she'd met at an event a few days earlier. They were having a "getting to know you" chat when she saw an opportunity to add some humor…

- Guy: *"I work for myself."*
- Harriet: *"Nice! So, what's your boss like? Haha."*
- Guy: *"No you didn't hear me, I work for myself."*
- Harriet: *"I heard you, I meant… well, my dad's favorite joke is that he hates the self check-out line because he always gets the worst checker."*
- Guy: *"Maybe your dad meant the people in line were the worst."*
- Harriet: *"Um, no."*

Should Harriet have stopped pursuing things with this guy because of that misfire? Not necessarily; but humor is a huge part of any relationship, so it's something to keep in mind during the dating process. Most people want a partner who can make them laugh, not one who they have to explain their jokes to.

If your sense of humor falls flat with someone, create your own little moment and enjoy it yourself. Here are some lines I've used to follow up on some of my jokes that elicited anything other than a positive response…

- *"Okydoky then."*
- *"Well, I thought it was funny."*
- *"Great, thanks for playing!"*

Saying anything along those lines as a follow-up to radio silence or a weird look after sharing your humor naturally closes-up the interaction, so you can confidently move on to the next one.

#2 Set + Keep a Similar Tone

The second key aspect of being consistent is to keep generally the same tone. This applies to my earlier example of a woman at a networking event trying too hard to create a great first impression by talking in a higher-pitched tone. Instead of doing that (please… just don't), simply speak in the normal tone that you'd use when talking to your mom or your best friend – starting with the first word that comes out of your mouth.

Forcing any excitement outside of how you truly feel is going to feel uncomfortable and come off as disingenuous to the person you're talking to. It's also exhausting to keep up that level of faux energy for the rest of the conversation. Once you start in a high tone, how do you transition to talking in a normal tone?

Important Note on Cultural Differences

"At the end of the day, if you're gay, straight, black, white, it doesn't matter who you are… truly all people want to connect."
    – Jonathan Van Ness, *Queer Eye*

Women from dozens of different countries have reached out to me asking how to navigate the cultural nuances in their corner of the world – e.g. "In Sweden strangers don't talk to each other," and "In Indonesia, people think you're weird if you smile at them."

I always respond the same: cultural customs may be different, but at the end of the day we're all still human, which means we all have the same fundamental needs of acceptance, appreciation, and love. I've dated men from all across the world and traveled to over thirty different countries, so I've seen first-hand these universal desires of people across many different cultures, ethnicities, and religions – as well as a broad range of different ages, professions, and personalities.

Maybe in your culture, it's considered weird to talk to strangers, but you personally love chatting-up people you meet on the street. I encourage you to do what feels right for *you* and to trust that even if most people around you are conforming to the non-chat norm, the right ones will be open to connecting with you – and that's all you need. Just that one person who sees your willingness to connect and thinks, "Finally, someone else who likes to meet new people!" That's your person, and it's often worth pushing through perceived social norms to find him.

Just be sure you're not breaking any local laws or putting yourself in a situation that could be dangerous. Always use your best judgment and knowledge of each circumstance, especially if you're in a place where women don't (yet) have the same rights and freedoms as men do.

The same goes for when you're traveling the world and want to connect with people in different countries, or even different states within the U.S. Enter every interaction with a genuine intention and love of connection and trust the right people will find you because of that.

The lesson with this is that no matter where you live always stay true to yourself and what feels right for you. If you want to chat up a stranger or connect deeply with someone, chances are there are other people within arm's reach of you who want the same thing, but they may not know how or have your same skills or courage to go for it. But they'll be delighted when you do.

....

Hiding your need for connection will only prevent you from finding the people who can give it to you.

....

Action Item

1. What's one way you can treat a stranger the same way you would treat a close friend?

If He Initiates With You...

In this section, we'll cover what to do when a man tries to start a conversation with you. I'll give you simple scripts to respond to him in a way that feels comfortable and natural. In *Chapter III: Asked Out Organically*, I'll show you how to progress the conversation into more meaningful territory and then turn it into a date.

The Rules of Engagement

There are Five Rules of Engagement to keep in mind when a man kicks off a conversation with you. With these as your guide, you'll feel confident in handling any interaction a man initiates.

    Rule #1: Assume He's Interested
    Rule #2: Find the Positive
    Rule #3: Accept All Compliments
    Rule #4: Just Go With It
    Rule #5: Don't Be Cruel

Let's dive deeper into each of these...

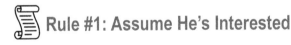 # Rule #1: Assume He's Interested

"Shall we all look for some ribbon together?"
    – Mr. Wickham to the Bennet sisters, *Pride and Prejudice* (2005)

If a man approaches you, assume he has an interest in you until proven otherwise; i.e. assume that you are a woman he finds attractive on some level. Chances are he's not interested in the weather, or looking for ribbon, or whatever other random topic he used as a reason to engage you. He's interested in *you,* my dear.

Here's an example: one of my workshop students, Maddy, had a pink crystal necklace that she wore almost every day. When I shared my tip about dressing for confidence and a conversation from the previous chapter, here's what she said…

- Maddy: *"Oh, I wear my pink crystal necklace everywhere and men always come up to me and comment on it."*
- Me: *"Perfect! How do you respond to keep the conversation going?"*
- Maddy: *"I say thanks and walk away…Oh. Shoot."*

We sent some gratitude to all the men who had approached Maddy using her pink crystal necklace as an excuse to engage her but had been unintentionally shot down because she was clueless.

Rule #2: Find the Positive

While there are general patterns across human behavior, layered on top of those are every person's unique personality, emotions, sense of humor, and other aspects that fluctuate day to day, even moment to moment.

If you find yourself not completely understanding what someone said to you or questioning the intention behind what they said, don't immediately jump to a negative conclusion. Always assume they meant it in the best possible way and then ask a question to clarify, like…

- *"What do you mean?"*
- *"Why is that?"*
- *"Tell me more about that."*

This "perceive as positive" approach will not only stop you from being offended by well-meaning (albeit slightly inarticulate) people, but questions like the examples above give the conversation a chance to go deeper, as opposed to moving on in the conversation while you secretly remain offended.

Defaulting to a positive assumption will change your general outlook on life in a great way. For instance, one afternoon a friend and I were on a luxury home tour and wandered into a room separate from the main area. Suddenly a woman came up to us and said…

"Excuse me, only models and caterers are supposed to be in here. Are you two models?"

We could have been offended or embarrassed, but since my default is to assume the positive, my first thought was "She asked if I was a model! Who cares if she was just being polite, that's awesome!" So I said…

"Nope, but thanks for thinking we might be!"

It turned a potentially awkward situation into a fun and flattering experience. I mean, who doesn't want to be mistaken for a model?

Another example is from the movie *Dumb and Dumber*. The main character, Harry, is attending a charity auction and walks up to a beautiful woman and says…

"Nice set of hooters you got there."

The woman turns to him with disdain and says…

"I beg your pardon?"

Then the camera zooms out and shows that they're standing in front of a pair of owls, the subject of the charity auction. Harry quickly clarifies…

"The owls, they're beautiful."

Lesson learned: ask clarifying questions before jumping to offense.

📜 Rule #3: Accept All Compliments

Accepting compliments can be challenging for many women because we've been taught to not "stray from the pack" and risk being seen as vain and/or different from everyone else in that moment.

One of my favorite exercises from my live workshops is when I ask each attendee to turn to the woman sitting next to her and give her a genuine compliment. The rule is that the woman receiving the compliment is not allowed to give one in return nor deflect it. She can only say "Thank you" and describe the complimented object and/or what the compliment meant to her (e.g. "Thank you, what a sweet thing to say!").

Since many women's knee-jerk reaction to a compliment is to immediately scramble to return the compliment, the first round of this exercise is always a little awkward. But after running through a few rounds, "Thank you" started to become the new comfortable default response as the ladies pushed past their fear of coming off as ungrateful and settled into simply receiving the kind words as a gift.

An example of this self-deprecating phenomenon taken to a hilarious extreme is the skit "Compliments" from the show *Inside Amy Schumer*. The scene is a series of female friends dishing out heartfelt compliments to each other... only to have each woman take the compliment she was given and turn it into an insult about herself. Here's one of the scripts:

- *Woman 1: "Oh my God Brie, you dyed your hair it looks amazing!"*
- *Woman 2: "Oh no you're just being nice."*
- *Woman 1: "No seriously it looks great."*
- *Woman 2: "No, I tried to look like Kate Hudson but ended up looking like a Golden Retriever's dingleberry."*

If your own natural reaction to a compliment is to immediately give one back or discount it, pause and think about how that feels when you do it. Probably not very good; or, as one of my clients, Emma, put it, "It feels like I'm just throwing away their compliment." Well said, Emma.

A good reframe is to visualize someone's compliment as them handing a physical gift to you. Would your first reaction be to immediately give it back to them – or take them to the place they bought it and return it right in front of them? Of course not. You'd simply say, "Thank you!" and accept it. So do the exact same thing with every compliment you receive.

As with gift-giving, the person paying the compliment almost always feels more joy from giving it than the person receiving it does. So if you struggle to receive kind words, start by accepting them for the sake of making the *other* person feel good.

Compliments can also serve as great icebreakers. The next time you receive a compliment, instead of saying, "Thanks!" which can feel awkward because it just hangs there, try describing the action or the topic that you were just gifted.

For example, if someone holds the door open for you, you could say…

- *"Thanks for holding the door open for me."*
- *"Well aren't you a gentleman. Thank you."*

Or tell a little story about whatever you were just complimented on. Maybe someone said they liked your bracelet; tell a short backstory on why or where you got it, and end with a question back to them to keep the conversation going. For instance:

- *"Thank you, I love vintage jewelry. What caught your eye about it?"*
- *"Are you into vintage jewelry too?"*
- *"Red's my favorite color – sounds like you're a fan too?"*

This hits the metaphorical conversation ball back to the other person and gives the interaction a direction to go in, without scrambling to find an immediate compliment to come back with.

Action Items

1. What's your general response when you receive a compliment?
2. Why do you think you react that way?
3. If you struggle with accepting compliments, choose a go-to compliment acceptance approach:
   - Describe the action or topic he complimented you on.
   - Or tell a little story about it (guides convo better).
   - Have a question to ask back after accepting a compliment.

 Rule #4: Just Go With It

Unless you're feeling a "something is seriously off with this guy" vibe, go with the flow of whatever he said so you can help him kick-off the conversation.

Imagine the situation from his perspective: he spots you, a woman he's attracted to, and wants to get your attention before he misses his chance. He's trying to think on his feet, so it's probably going to be a random topic. This is why in *Chapter I: Magnetic Approachability* we covered how to dress for confidence and a conversation so you provide something visual for him to easily comment on.

Another exercise I led my workshop attendees through illustrates how hard it is for a man to come up with something to say to a woman on the spot. I paired-up attendees, with one woman playing herself and the other woman wearing a male celebrity mask (David Beckham, Brad Pitt, Johnny Depp, Prince William, or Will.I.Am) to play the part of the man she encounters.

I then give each pair a scene – such as "Heidi is on the bus going to work, reading a book about a remote Amazonian tribe… when suddenly Prince William's twin sits down next to her – what can he say to get her attention?"

Not only does this allow the women to get comfortable thinking on their feet, but it also gives them a whole new appreciation with how nerve-wracking it can feel to approach someone and try to engage them without being too weird or creepy. It's also impossible to take yourself seriously when wearing these masks, which are about 30% larger than a normal face.

So remember, whatever a man says to engage you, as long as it isn't totally offensive, try to just go with it and help him out. He'll appreciate it and you can *both* benefit from getting the conversation party started.

Embrace the *"Yes, and..."*

A good mantra to keep in mind when talking to people you meet for the first time is the "Yes, and…" rule of improv comedy. That means whatever the other person says, you find some way to agree and/or build upon it to keep the conversation moving in a positive direction.

It's the same technique they use in the TV show *Whose Line Is It Anyway?* where comedians are given a scene, then work together in the moment to play it out. You'll never hear anyone shut down the skit by disagreeing with whatever random thing comes out of the other comedian's mouth. They always use the "Yes, and…" approach.

A real-life example of this was when I was in a drug store greeting aisle looking for a card for a friend's birthday when a man came up to me and said…

"Any good ones in there?"

Since my default response to strangers is the same as it is to my friends – and tends to involve humor – I said…

"Well, there are definitely some strange ones."

I then showed him the awkward card I was holding, we shared a laugh, and he ended up asking for my phone number.

Another example was at a charity event; I was standing by myself waiting for a friend to arrive when a woman I didn't know came up to me and said…

"Are you Christine's friend?"

I could have just said "No" and ended it there. But instead, I saw the opportunity to make a connection and said…

"Nope. But hi, I'm Camille. So who's Christine?"

The woman and I ended up hanging out the rest of the night and having a great time together.

I've also had men approach me with some seemingly random lines – many of which led to being asked out by them, because I knew exactly what was happening and just rolled with it…

Example 1

- Man #1: *"Do you know where the nearest pizza place is?"*
- Me: *"Not off the top of my head, but what kind of are you looking for?"*

Example 2

- Man #2: *"Did you catch the Blackhawks game last night?"*
- Me: *"I missed it, how'd they do?"*

So be on the lookout for those random comments and questions. Go beyond their face value and look at the possible intention behind them – then see where it goes!

Rule #5: Don't Be Cruel

Never put a man (or anyone) down – even if you're "joking." I used to do this to men I liked because I was scared they could see that I was interested in them; so I went to the extreme opposite in how I treated them. Not only did it feel awful, but it definitely didn't get me any dates.

Usually we "bring out the mean" when we're afraid of being rejected. It's easier to tell yourself that if you reject someone else first, then it doesn't matter if they reject you. But that approach only means that you're rejecting everyone, all the time, and never truly connecting with anyone. Later in this chapter, I'll show you how to overcome the most common fears around initiating a conversation.

Sometimes people can be short or defensive as a default reaction to someone who simply caught them off-guard. Refer to *Chapter I: Magnetic Approachability* on the importance of doing a quick scan of every place you step into, so you can spot men before they approach you and thus feel safer when they do.

If your sense of humor is more on the sarcastic side, lead with the kindest part of that until you and the person you just met get to know each other a little more, so they can tell when you're joking versus being serious.

Also, try to find something to continue the conversation that feels genuinely interesting to you. I'm not a sports fan, so I'll never start an interaction off on a lie pretending to be interested in sports. But whenever that topic comes up in random conversations (especially when I know it's simply being used to engage me) I'll find something positive in it while still being honest, such as…

- *"I don't follow sports closely, but I always enjoy a live game."*
- *"I'm not big on sports, but I like movies about sports."*

If You Initiate With Him...

So what happens when you want to initiate a conversation with a man? Here are the Rules of Engagement to help *you* break the ice with anyone…

The Rules of Engagement

Rule #1: You Can Totally Initiate
Rule #2: Choose Easy + Relatable
Rule #3: Skip the Formalities
Rule #4: Opportunity > Outcome
Rule #5: Prepare For Rain

Rule #1: You Can Totally Initiate

Some women insist that the man should always make the first move – but I disagree. What if you see him but he doesn't see you yet? Or he can't read your signals that you want him to approach you?

Waiting for the man to always initiate means you'll miss a lot of opportunities, so permission granted to make the first move yourself. In this section, I'll show you how to do it without risk of rejection.

Because sometimes you just get one chance to connect with someone before they disappear forever. You don't want to walk away from a situation thinking, "I should have said something to him, what if he was meant to be in my life?" or "I should have just asked him about his Maroon 5 shirt, he was so cute!" or "We kept locking eyes from across the lobby, but I didn't know what to do next."

Avoid any painful regret by finding the courage to take action in the moment. Just make sure at some point he starts to take the lead in the conversation so it's confirmed that he's interested in you too.

Rule #2: Choose Easy + Relatable

The best icebreaker topics are simply drawn from the situation around you. People need to have instant context for the random phrase or question you just shared with them in order for them to pick up the conversation ball – so keep it clear and simple.

Use whatever is around you in the moment so it's relevant to the other person too. Here are some examples…

Day of the week
- Icebreaker: *"TGIF!"*
- Follow-up to icebreaker: *"Heck yeah! How's your Friday going?"*

Holiday
- Icebreaker: *"Happy New Year."*
- Follow-up to icebreaker: *"You too! Any resolutions for this one?"*

Weather
- Icebreaker: *"Gorgeous weather, right?"*
- Follow-up to icebreaker: *"It's awesome. Any plans to take advantage?"*

People
- Icebreaker: *"Did that guy just do a handstand against that stop sign?"*
- Follow-up to icebreaker: *"Yep, he sure did. Just keepin' it real, right?"*

Clothes / Accessories
- Icebreaker: *"Your watch is very unique, I like it."*
- Follow-up to icebreaker: *"Thanks, I just got it. I have a thing for watches, how about you?"*

Objects
- Icebreaker: *"Is that brand of bagel bites any good?"*
- Follow-up to icebreaker: *"They're delicious, the perfect mix of sweet and salty. Are you a lover of the bites too?"*

This is why I don't recommend having one universal "pre-planned" line to open every conversation because it will feel forced, likely be out of context for most situations, and create confusion instead of a conversation.

Asking a question gives you control over which topic you start the conversation on, so choose one that you genuinely like or are curious about. For example, if it's Friday you might be thinking…

> *"Yay it's Friday! What am I curious about right now? Well, it's my favorite day of the week, and I have exciting plans with Aaliyah this weekend. I wonder what plans this other person has for the weekend…"*

And then ask them! Using everyday topics like this will keep your investment (and thus risk of rejection) next to nothing. It also gives the other person the chance to either opt-in or opt-out of continuing the conversation.

Also, note that these topics are simply for purposes of breaking the ice – you shouldn't talk about these surface-level subjects for more than a minute or two. They simply serve as a safe way to kick off a connection in a way that's comfortable and inviting. Toward the end of this chapter, I'll show you four simple words to steer every conversation off the random icebreaker and into a more meaningful connection.

Rule #3: Skip the Formalities

When you break the ice with someone, don't make it a formal affair. Using perfectly proper language and/or a stiff tone only serves to make the conversation feel distanced and business-like.

....

Remember: if you wouldn't say it to your best friend,
don't say it to a stranger.

....

For instance, one of my clients Stephanie was headed to a blues bar with live music and wanted to practice meeting new people. She walked me through her previous attempt to engage people there, which was to sit down next to someone, introduce herself, and then… have no clue what to say next.

I pointed out that she wouldn't go through that formal introduction approach with a friend; she'd simply turn to them and share an offhand thought or question about the band or the venue or whatever she was genuinely interested in at the moment. So I recommended she take that same approach with strangers too, and to say something like…

- *"This is my first time seeing this band live, how about you?"*
- *"What's your favorite song of theirs?"*
- *"Such a great way to spend a Friday night, right?"*

Formally introducing yourself to someone leaves the conversation without a purpose or a next direction to go in and can get uncomfortable *real quick*. Instead, make a comment or ask a question to kick things off, which gives the conversation a clear purpose and introduces a relatable topic that the other person can instantly contribute to. Then later in the conversation you can say, "By the way, I'm Camille…" and the introduction will feel like a natural part of the already-great conversation.

Rule #4: Opportunity > Outcome

"Luck is where preparation meets opportunity."
  – Seneca, Roman philosopher

Another one of my clients wanted to practice talking to men, so she hit the town by herself and made an evening of it. But when we debriefed about it the next day she said, "I talked to three attractive men, but none of them asked me out. The night was a total failure."

I reminded her that a few weeks ago she had felt too shy to talk to *anyone* – let alone a man she was attracted to – so the fact that she had gone out by herself and talked to three men in one night was fantastic! The outcome didn't matter. I was so proud of her for pushing her comfort zone and finding her conversation flow; nothing about that was a failure.

You will never truly know what's going on with someone in the moment you meet them. You also can't control them or the outcome of your interaction. So release those expectations as soon as you feel them setting in.

Personally, I love to feel in control of myself and my life as much as possible. Yet I've discovered there's incredible freedom in accepting that I can't control another person because that means I don't have to be responsible for them. How exhausting would it be if you were in charge of not only yourself but everyone else you came in contact with? Ugh, no thanks.

You can, and *should,* be prepared for random interactions by presenting your real self to the world, smiling at strangers, making eye contact, etc. But after covering those basics, it's up to the other person to determine if they want to start or continue engaging with you.

Ironically, when you release the need to control and/or achieve a specific outcome from an interaction and instead focus on simply enjoying it, *that* is often what makes a man feel comfortable and inspired to ask you out. More on how to do that in *Chapter III: Asked Out Organically.*

A simple hack to get out of your head and into the conversation is to pretend that every interaction with a man is simply "practice for the next one." This will help take your focus off trying to force a certain outcome since you're "just practicing."

A Quick to Get Fast Results

If you've been filling out the Action Items in the book, well done! Now I invite you to take the next step and grab my FREE Offline Dating Method Experiential Workbook. The workbook contains all Action Items from the book gathered in one convenient resource with space to fill out your answers. It also has dozens of bonus exercises not found in the book to accelerate your results. Just go to **www.OfflineDatingMethod.com**.

Rule #5: Prepare For Rain

As you're out and about practicing your engagement skills, there may be some people who try to rain on your conversation parade. If that happens, remember their reaction is 100% about them and not about you. They don't even *know* you, so you literally can't take whatever they said personally.

Maybe you simply caught them off-guard or maybe you're the first person who's shown them kindness in a long time. Assume their less-than-optimal reaction is due to one of those reasons and be proud of yourself for giving the gift of acknowledgment to someone who probably needed it – even if you don't see the positive ways it affected them. Pretend it ended up being the highlight of their day once they finally realized what just happened.

Remember, the worst-case scenario when attempting to engage someone isn't even that bad. So what, you get a blank stare or no response from a stranger? Is that going to ruin your week? Girl, please. No way.

Overcoming the Four Fears

F.E.A.R. = **F**alse **E**vidence **A**ppearing **R**eal

Speaking of fear, it's completely normal to feel some anxiety about the prospect of talking to strangers – especially if you're a little out of practice. Through my own experiences as well as my clients, I've found four common fears that tend crop-up at this point in the connection process:

- Fear of Rejection
- Fear of Being Awkward
- Fear of Being Creepy
- Fear He's Already Taken

The way to move past each of these fears is to disprove it. This can be done by looking for evidence that supports *the opposite* of what you're afraid of using the people and situations around you.

When your fear goes unquestioned or unproven for too long, it can grow to massive proportions and lodge in your head as a "fact." For example, an initial thought like "I can't talk to people I don't know because they might think I'm weird," put on repeat in your head every day for years can easily turn into "When I talk to strangers they think I'm a weirdo," and subconsciously accepting it as truth.

To move past this, first start to question those anxieties by asking yourself, "What am I *truly* afraid of when talking to people?" The more you understand where your fear is coming from, the more you start to challenge it. Next, ask yourself what's the worst that might actually happen if you played out the scenario you're afraid of. I guarantee it's not going to be that bad. This simple exercise of naming the fear and then thinking of the most terrifying outcome possible (which won't actually be possible) gives the fear less power and enables you to start dispelling it.

Next, take small steps to prove to yourself that those fears won't happen – such as starting a conversation with someone (I'll show you how in a minute) and experiencing that your worst fear doesn't actually happen. The goal here is to prove your fear wrong by creating new experiential memories that support the outcome you desire – i.e. the opposite of what you've been afraid would happen.

> Overcome your negative fear by creating an experience
> that proves the positive opposite of it.

By creating a new experience like this, you're replacing formerly negative emotions associated with it with new positive emotions. Humans change their behavior on an emotional level, not a logical level. That's why experiencing a situation that disproves your fear is one-thousand times more effective in dispelling it than trying to logically reason it away.

Plus, whatever your worst fear is around talking to someone, I can almost guarantee it will never happen. After years of proving wrong my own debilitating fears with engaging people, I've now spoken with thousands of strangers and the worst thing that's ever happened was a few people didn't acknowledge me. Whoop-de-doo.

Next, let's dive into the four most common engagement fears and techniques to quickly overcome them, so you feel empowered to push past them and start initiating great conversations.

Fear of Rejection

"It is only ONE person's opinion. There are seven billion people in the world and everyone has opinions; most of which are an instinctual response to being presented with new stimulus – which means it is more about them than it is you."

– Jesse Krieger, my wise publisher

The best way to overcome this fear is by using my Friendly or Flirting Technique, which is when you simply talk to everyone the same way you would a friend. When you say something casual to a man, such as, "I love your leather bag, what a great shade of camel!" he has no clue if you're saying it because you want to engage him or if you simply love his bag and wanted to share that.

This technique lowers the fear of rejection for both you and him – and when you *decrease* the fear of rejection, you *increase* the chance of engagement. It's the same concept you discovered in *Chapter I: Magnetic Approachability.*

Another example: let's say you're standing in the snack aisle of the grocery store and spot a cute guy a few feet away who's reading the back of a box of granola bars. Ask yourself: "If he was a woman and I had a question about those granola bars, what would I say?" Then simply say the exact same thing to him.

> If you don't know what to say to a man, just ask "What would I say to a woman?" and say that to him.

Here are a few options for that scenario:

- *"What's that brand you're holding?"*
- *"Are those any good? I haven't tried them…"*
- *"Do those have almonds in them?"* (bonus points because this gives him a task to check the ingredients, and men love feeling helpful)

Those are instantly relatable questions that have a purpose, are easy to answer, and require minimal investment from both you and him. If his response to any of those lines involves a weird look or if he answers your question then promptly walks away, so what? Your stake in the interaction was so minimal that it won't even faze you. Next, please!

My client Veronica had a similar situation in the bread aisle at Trader Joe's. She and her friend were standing about fifteen feet apart when Veronica found the bread she was looking for and called out, "Hey, Anna! I found my favorite bread, you're gonna love it – it's very buttery."

A man who was standing in between them turned to Veronica and immediately asked "Which bread?" and they started chatting. His question might have been just an excuse to engage her – or he may have honestly just wanted a new bread to try. Who knows, who cares? They ended up connecting in a random place and enjoying the moment together.

Fear of Being Awkward

If you have a fear of saying something awkward, chances are you've over-compensated for that by trying to think of the perfect line so it will come out "more naturally." The unfortunate irony with this approach is that by taking the time to craft a "more natural" sentence you completely strip it of being natural, which will make it feel and sound even *more* awkward.

> The longer you hesitate to say something,
> the bigger your fear of saying it will grow.

The quickest way to overcome this fear is to use my Mind to Mouth Move. To apply it, catch the first thought that pops in your head about the person you want to engage with, then say it out loud to them before you give yourself the chance to overthink it. In other words, take your first thought immediately from your *mind* to your *mouth*.

This prevents you from over-rehearsing what to say and ultimately psyching yourself out from saying it. Over time, practicing this technique will build trust in yourself that whatever you end up saying, it will do the job just fine.

So maybe you have a thought like, "Wow, I love that woman's scarf. I wonder where she got it." Immediately go over to her and say, "Excuse me, I love your scarf. Where'd you get it?"

Do not hesitate. Do not try to re-word. Do not talk yourself out of it. And always keep whatever you share *positive*.

When you make it a habit to say it as soon as it pops in your head, your fear doesn't have the chance to creep in. The more you practice this, the faster you'll get. Plus, you'll continually prove to yourself that, overall, people are very receptive to talking to you – and it's fun!

Fear of Being Creepy

While this may feel like a valid fear, let me point out that it's difficult for a woman to come across as creepy. Not impossible, but difficult. For better or for worse, the word "creep" is socially coded to men. Sorry guys.

For example, if a woman brushes up against a man's leg in the middle of a conversation, chances are he's not going to feel disrespected or violated. If a man does that to a woman, he will likely be labeled a creep. Yes, it's a double-standard, but it is what it is.

Being creepy usually boils down to not respecting someone's personal space or lingering too long past the point of when an interaction would have naturally come to a close.

So as long as you're not running your hands all over every person you meet and you're paying attention to basic social cues, take heart that, as a female, you are more than likely far from coming across as a creep. I'll show you how to know when it's time to leave a conversation – and how to do it – in *Chapter III: Asked Out Organically*.

Fear He's Already Taken

This is a respectable fear in that you don't want to overstep your bounds if a man you find attractive is off the market. The problem with this is that, other than wearing a wedding ring or having a woman on his arm, it's impossible to know if a man is "taken" or not by simply looking at him.

The best way to find out if a man is single is to engage him and see where he takes the connection.

By being your authentic self with everyone, you're simply starting conversations with fellow humans about everyday topics. It's not disrespectful to acknowledge a man or ask him a question, no matter what his relationship status is. I would even argue that it's prejudiced to purposefully *avoid* talking to a man simply because he has a wedding ring on. Married men need human connection too!

Use the eleven easy icebreakers (coming up) to engage him in a casual question, comment, or compliment. Then wait for a signal that he's interested in continuing the conversation. Because it *is* his responsibility to let you know at some point that he's taken. You're not a mind reader.

When you choose not to engage with a man because you're afraid he's already taken, you are making the decision for him that he wouldn't enjoy a conversation with you. That's not fair to him, and I don't want you hindering your own pursuit of a great partner for the sake of that tiny risk.

That's like chatting up someone at a party, offering to grab them a glass of wine, and having them respond that they don't drink alcohol. So what? You were just being nice and had no way of knowing that. Would a moment like that prevent you from ever offering another person a glass of wine again? Of course not, you had only good intentions.

If a man you're chatting with suddenly brings up a girlfriend or wife in the middle of your conversation, no need to get embarrassed. Again, how were you supposed to know? Instead, *purposefully incorporate her into the conversation*. Ask what her name is, or my personal go-to would be to ask how they met. I always love those stories.

Taking this approach to acknowledge his significant other will not only feel more respectful and less awkward in the moment, but it'll also empower you to chat-up any man because if he happens to reveal his relationship mid-conversation, you know exactly how to handle it.

Action Items

1. What's the #1 barrier preventing you from talking to strangers?
2. What's your underlying fear behind it?
3. What's the worst that might happen if you talk to a stranger?
4. What are the actual chances that will ever happen?
5. What advice would you give to a friend who had that fear?

Eleven Super Simple Ways to Start a Conversation

Know what time it is? Icebreaker time! Below are eleven different approaches you can use to start a conversation with absolutely anyone.

As you read through them, pick the approach that feels the most comfortable for you. The topic of conversation will change depending on the situation you're in, but the general approaches will work the same way across every interaction.

#1 Pull a RAOK

You can never go wrong with a Random Act of Kindness (RAOK), regardless of how the recipient responds. It's a great way to break through your fear of talking to people because it makes the interaction more about them than about you.

An example of a RAOK might be putting your umbrella over someone else while you're both walking down the street in the same direction or saying, "Bless you!" when a stranger sneezes.

One of my favorite RAOK examples happened on a train ride home from work one night. It was crowded with rush-hour commuters, but when a new batch of people got on, I saw a man stand up from his seat and offer it to a woman. She smiled and accepted; the man beamed with pride. But he didn't stop there.

At the next stop, another seat became available, so the man tapped the shoulder of a different woman who was standing and pointed to the free seat. She mouthed, "Thank you" and sat down. This cycle continued for the next few stops, and at each stop, a new seat or two would open up and Captain Save-A-Seat would find a woman and offer it to her. I watched as he lit up with more and more joy after every successful seat placement and ended up starting a conversation with one of the grateful women.

If you can channel even an ounce of that same kindness and enjoyment into your encounters with people throughout your day, you're going to become addicted to how fulfilling it feels to make other people feel good.

#2 Drop a Compliment

We've already covered several ways to give a compliment, but here's one more that is just two words: "nice" (or "cool," or "interesting," or whatever word feels authentic for you) and then fill in the blank with whatever you're complimenting – shirt, socks, watch, the thing you genuinely like.

It's possible to connect to any man in just two words:
"Nice_____ [watch / shirt / socks / etc]."

You can, of course, expand on this technique as well, for example...

- You: *"Great cufflinks. What's the symbol on them?"*
- Guy: *"Thanks! My family is from England and it's our coat of arms."*
- You: *"Very cool. What part of England are they from?"*

Boom! You just went from the topic of cufflinks to talking about his family's 300-year-old estate in Cornwall in less than ten seconds. Just make sure the compliment is authentic; otherwise, you'll feel out of alignment the moment you say it and start the interaction off with a lie. When in doubt, if you want to use an object as an icebreaker but it's not completely to your taste, just say it's "interesting" or that it "caught your eye."

#3 Change It Up

How often do you find yourself being asked, "How are you?" as you go about your day? If your default response is like most people's, it's along the lines of, "Good, how are you?" Which means it's basically an endless cycle of... well, nothing of any substance.

Instead, try responding to standard greetings and questions in a different way. So when you're next asked, "How are you?" you might say…

- *"I am absolutely fabulous. How are you?"*
- *"Meh, it's Monday. Let's talk about the weekend – got any fun plans?"*
- *"Just another day trying to save the world. How about you?"*

You can do this in showing your gratitude too. Instead of saying "Thanks" when someone does something nice for you, try…

- *"Gracias"*
- *"Danke"*
- *"Merci"*

Even if you don't speak those languages, everyone knows what they mean; at least the right people for you do, and that's all that matters.

It's a small shift that can create a very different type of conversation. Again, be authentic with how you're truly feeling. If you aren't having the best day, don't say that you're feeling fabulous – but find something positive to share such as, "I'm just glad it's finally Friday!"

#4 Casually Cut-In

When you overhear an interesting conversation in public, permission granted to chime in about it – again, as long as you keep it positive. Then give the other person or people a little space to see if they bring you into the interaction.

My general rule is that if someone is talking about a topic in public, it's open for (positive) public comment. Taking this approach has even led to me being asked out on a date. I was in my building's lobby checking the mail and around the corner a man was talking to the doorman about a bad date he'd just come back from. So, of course, my ears perked up when he said the word "date". I walked over to them and chimed in with, "Ooo, I love bad date stories. What happened?" He shared the story (yep, it was bad) and at the end of it said to me, "Wanna go grab a drink right now?" and we headed out on a spontaneous date together!

#5 Sprinkle Some Value

This is related to the Mind to Mouth Move in that if you see something or someone who piques your interest, share your thoughts with them. That could be suggesting your favorite seasonal drink to the man in line behind you at Starbucks who just said, "I have no idea what to order" – or asking someone who looks completely lost if you can help them.

My friend, Beverly, met her husband while sitting in a coffee shop reading a book on Buddhism. She caught his eye and her book made it easy for him to approach say, "I'm into Buddhism too. Mind if I sit with you?" Heck, you can even use *this* book as a conversation starter with its unconventional title and unique colors.

Other examples where you can showcase your expertise or add value could be when volunteering at a homeless shelter and sharing tips with the new guy on how to serve the meals. Or maybe you spot a man who's wearing a shirt from your favorite sports team and, still excited from their win last night, you say, "That was such a great game – grand slam!" and use that mutual interest as a way to engage him.

A great warm-up to this approach is doing what I call an "advice drop." Go ahead and drop some unsolicited positive advice or a recommendation on a stranger, then just keep on walking. Don't even wait for the other person to respond, which will take the pressure off you to continue the conversation.

#6 Share a Short Quip

Use the Mind to Mouth Move to share a random observation or showcase your humor out loud to no one in particular. Look for what I call a "shared moment" – where something unusual or noteworthy happens and everyone who witnessed it sort of looks around at each other with the expression, "Did anyone else just see that?" Sharing a short quip takes those situations a step further because you're saying out loud what everyone else is likely thinking.

For example, one Halloween I was riding the bus to a friend's house and for some reason, the bus had a very strange vibe. Maybe it was because of the holiday and some people were in costumes, but others were just acting plain bizarre. After a few minutes of noticing this, I finally turned to the woman next to me and said, "This is the weirdest bus ride I've ever been on." She immediately responded with, "Oh thank God, I was thinking the same thing!"

#7 Spread the News

As with everything, make any topic that you use as an icebreaker one that you genuinely care about. Maybe you're sitting on the train, scrolling through *The New York Times* and feel inspired to turn to the man next to you and say, "They just found the missing hiker, alive!" If you're into sports, ask the woman standing next to you in the elevator, "Did you catch the Bulls win last night?"

This approach works for anything newsworthy that most people will likely have some instant context on. My personal suggestion: stay on neutral topics instead of getting political.

#8 Try a "Hi"

This approach is just one word and four quick steps: catch a man's eye, flash him a smile, say, "Hi," and then go back to doing whatever you were doing.

1. Catch a man's eye
2. Flash a smile
3. Say *"Hi!"*
4. Continue doing whatever you were doing.

In just *one word*, you're showing him that...

- You saw him.
- You're a nice person.
- You're open to chatting.

That's a flashing green light for him to approach you! This approach is perfect for when you find yourself exchanging glances with a man and wondering, "Is he going to say something? Do I say something? What the hell do I do now?" Just say, "Hi!" and break the sound barrier by cutting through the silent tension and open the door for him to engage you.

#9 Ask a Question

Use the elements around you to get curious and ask a question. For instance, one time I was waiting for a friend at a Mexican restaurant for Cinco de Mayo. I saw a cute guy next to me at the bar, so I engaged him...

- Me: *"What are you drinking?"*
- Guy: *"A margarita."*
- Me: *"Oh, is it good?"*
- Guy: *"Yeah, let me buy you your first margarita."*

The interaction could have ended at his first answer, but I went further and became curious, asking if it was good with the intention of, "I'm thinking about getting one myself. Did you enjoy it? Is it awful? Tell me about your margarita experience..." It was just a simple follow-up question that inspired him to buy me a drink!

There are always questions to be asked in any situation, so use your circumstances to get curious:

- At a charity event: *"What's your connection to the cause?"*
- At a concert: *"How do you feel about their new album?"*
- At a party: *"How do you know the birthday boy?"*

If you're out with a friend, another option to engage a man is to ask him to take a picture of you and your friend. Not only will that break the ice, but you'll give him the chance to stare at your gorgeous face a little longer. After he snaps the picture you can say, "Thank you. How's your day going?"

In *Chapter III: Asked Out Organically*, I'll give you the best questions to ask once you're in a conversation to keep it interesting and naturally flowing.

#10 Put In a Request

Men love being useful, it helps them bond with women and fulfills their desire to feel needed on a primal level. So even though you can do any and everything for yourself (you independent woman you), it's a great icebreaker to ask a man to do it for you. Plus, he'll love it. For example:

- On the bus: *"Can you tell me what the next stop is?"*
- At the bar: *"Can you ask the bartender for a glass of water please?"*
- In an elevator: *"Could you hit the tenth-floor button for me?"*

Purposefully asking a guy to do things for you is a great way to kick off a conversation. It also helps you become comfortable with a man helping you and shows that you have space for him in your life.

#11 Make Someone Smile

If you want to create an instant bond with someone, say something to make them smile. Get creative! People love laughing and lord knows the world needs more of that these days. Smile at random people, give a compliment, or make a funny observation out loud to no one in particular but within earshot of someone.

Action Items

1. Choose one of the eleven approaches to start a random convo:
   #1 Pull a RAOK
   #2 Drop a Compliment
   #3 Change It Up
   #4 Casually Cut-In
   #5 Sprinkle Some Value
   #6 Share a Short Quip
   #7 Spread the News
   #8 Try a "Hi"
   #9 Ask a Question
   #10 Put In a Request
   #11 Make Someone Smile
2. Why does that approach feel the most comfortable for you?

How to Keep it Going – Or Shut It Down

No matter which icebreaker approach you choose, eventually that topic will die out and present you with two options for what to do next:

1. Take the connection to a deeper level (and potentially a date)
2. End the conversation

The Four-Word Transition to Meaningful

If you'd like to keep the conversation going, you have to take it to a deeper level. Use one of these short segues to get off the small talk and into more meaningful territory:

- *"How's your day going?"*
- *"Where are you headed?"*
- *"Good event so far?"*

This is the safest and simplest way to shift into a more personal topic. It also helps confirm the other person's level of interest in continuing the conversation by letting them answer with as much or as little information as they prefer.

For instance, maybe a man approached you and complimented your shoes. Using your Four-Word Transition of choice will reveal if he was truly interested in them (maybe he wants a pair for his sister) or if he was using them as an excuse to talk to you.

Action Items

1. Choose a new go-to transition to get off the icebreaker topic:
   - *"How's your day going?"*
   - *"Where are you headed?"*
   - *"Good event so far?"*
   - Create one of your own (it doesn't have to be exactly four words, just keep it short and casual)
2. Give one reason why you genuinely care about that question.

Death of a Conversation

A big part of building your confidence in starting conversations is by knowing exactly how to end them. It's never fun to feel stuck talking to someone who couldn't care less that you're bored out of your mind.

However, you should only shut down a conversation if there's a legitimate reason – such as: if something seems off with the person, you gave the conversation your best shot but it's still bad, or the other person isn't actively engaging in it with you. Don't shut it down simply because you're nervous.

Here are some simple ways to exit a conversation…

If you can bolt quickly (e.g. no tab to pay off)**:**
- *"Well, it was nice chatting with you, gotta run!"*
- *"Have a good day!"*

If you're unable to distance yourself (e.g. he's sitting next to you on a plane, or you're in a rideshare pool with him)**:**
- *"I've had a bad day and I need to be alone right now."*
- *"I've got a headache, so I'm going to listen to some music."*

If he is clearly interested in you, but you know 100% you will never return that interest:
- *"My boyfriend loves that [sports team/state/beer type/whatever]!"*

If he asked you out:
- *"Thank you, I'm flattered, but I have a boyfriend."*

If he persists:
- *"I'm going to move seats if you don't stop bothering me."*

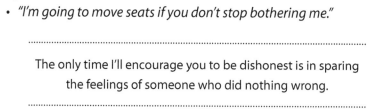

The only time I'll encourage you to be dishonest is in sparing the feelings of someone who did nothing wrong.

If you find yourself in a conversation with a man who's clearly interested in you but you don't return that interest, or you're simply not in the mood to talk, insert the word "boyfriend" into the conversation, even if it's not true. This can be a not-so-subtle, but kind way of saying, "I'm not interested, but I don't want to hurt your feelings by explicitly saying that so I'm going to give us both an easy out here."

There's always the option to go the brutally honest route by telling him that you're not interested – however, be prepared for a debate. Plus, that direct approach runs the risk of escalating if he takes your honesty as a personal insult, and sometimes it's just not worth the risk of provoking someone who might be dangerous.

Action Item

1. Choose one of the ways to end a conversation from the options above (or create your own).

Essential Engagement Extras

Next up, I'll show you a few more tips to help hone your conversation skills and make every engagement even easier (and way more fun).

- Four Ways to Never Forget Someone's Name Again
- Nine Actions to Gain Social Momentum
- How to Handle "One of Those Days"

Four Ways to Never Forget Someone's Name Again

"Remember: a person's name is, to that person, the sweetest sound in any language."
        – Dale Carnegie, *How to Win Friends and Influence People*

Forgetting someone's name after building a great connection with them can, unfortunately, damage the bond you just created.

Avoid those repercussions by choosing a go-to approach from the options below so you can remember a person's name the moment they give it to you. You never know if that man you chatted-up at your friend's party is going to be in your life for fifteen minutes or fifty years. So make it a habit to learn someone's name as soon as they share it.

Bonus tip: Make it a point to say the other person's name at least once in the middle of your conversation. Not only will it show you cared enough to learn it, but the act of saying it out loud will make them light up and feel instantly closer to you. Plus, it will further plant it within your memory. In

Chapter III: Asked Out Organically, I'll show you four ways to recover from forgetting someone's name mid-conversation.

But first, here are four ways to remember a person's name as soon as they share it with you, so you won't need the recovery methods. Choose the approach that resonates most with you and your learning style, then use it every time a new person introduces themselves to you.

#1 Associate It With Someone You Know (or Know of)

Did that intriguing guy at your friend's birthday party just introduce himself as Will? Immediately picture Will Smith, Will Ferrell, or any other Will of choice who you're familiar with. Just make it a Will who you have positive or neutral feelings about, so you don't immediately associate this new guy with "Scum of the Earth Ex-Boyfriend Will."

Visualize the face of already-familiar Will and create an emotional association between him and this new Will. By referencing unfamiliar new Will with familiar celebrity Will or friend Will, you are more likely to remember new Will's name – as well as your favorite Will Smith movie.

#2 Visualize It Spelled Out

Did you just meet a Sarah? Visually spell out her name in your mind: S-A-R-A-H.

Hmmm, I wonder if she spells it with an "h" on the end or not? For bonus points, show Sarah that you care about getting her name right and ask her that same question. I guarantee no one, except maybe her doctor's office, has ever asked her about the spelling, so you'll be instantly memorable to her *and* get the information you need to remember her name.

If you can't visualize someone's name because it's uncommon or hard to pronounce, ask them to spell it out letter by letter and visualize each letter as they do so. This will secure it in your mind because you're not only visualizing it, you're creating an experience in the process. Plus, they'll instantly love you for paying such close attention to their favorite word.

#3 Repeat It Right Back

As soon as someone shares their name, immediately repeat it out loud back to them a little bit slower.

- Woman: *"Hi, I'm Chelsea"*
- You: *"Chelsea, great to meet you. I'm Camille."*

This approach also helps when someone's name is hard to pronounce, and you get those bonus rapport points for showing them that you care enough to get it right.

#4 Create a Convention

If you're a creative type, come up with a fun naming convention for the name. Maybe you meet Stacy who's wearing a lace collar – she's now, "Stacy with the lacy." Or maybe you met Blaire while sitting in the red chair.

One of my best friends has the beautiful Greek name Ariadne. It's not a common name in the U.S., so when she introduces herself to a new person, they often struggle to pronounce it correctly. So I lovingly came up with a naming convention to help them out because, hey, I'm a good friend like that. Here's the breakdown:

- Letter "R"
- Letter "E"
- Odd (as in *weird*)
- Knee

Ariadne! It may be strange, but it gives people a fun and effective way to remember how to pronounce her name. And despite her laughing at me every time I go through it with a new person, it works. So there.

Action Items

1. Choose one of the four ways to remember people's name as soon as you meet them:

   #1 Associate it with someone you know or know of.

   #2 Visualize it when they say it to you.

   #3 Repeat it back to them when they say it.

   #4 Create a naming convention.

2. Why is that approach the most comfortable for you?

Nine Actions to Gain Social Momentum

When it comes to social interactions, momentum is the name of the game. The key is to start with a baby step that's easy and comfortable, get a small "win" under your belt, and then take the next step, and the next one.

The first time you try anything new, whether social skills-related or not, it's probably going to feel a little awkward. That's expected, it's new! But as you keep practicing and do it a second time, a third time, a fourth time, you'll quickly get into the momentum, find your natural groove, and start having fun with it.

Break through your conversation fears
by taking small steps to gain social momentum.

As we covered at the beginning of this chapter, social skills are like muscles and practicing these conversation starters is like getting in a great workout. If you hit the gym once, will you see any results? No. If you create a routine to go every Monday, Wednesday, and Friday morning before work, are you going to see results after just a few weeks? Definitely.

That said, here are nine actions that will get you into your effortless engagement flow:

#1 Add Some Acknowledgment

"You're never too important to be nice to people."
    – Jon Batiste, American musician

Today people crave not only connection but simple acknowledgment. Every person wants to feel like they matter in some way. Think of a time where you felt truly seen by someone and how amazing that felt. Now think of a time when you were completely ignored or disrespected and how that made you feel.

Many people have a deep-seated fear of becoming irrelevant – such as, "If I were to disappear tomorrow, would anyone notice?" My godfather shared that after retirement he stayed on several company boards, not for the money, but – as he put it – "to remain relevant."

So as you practice these engagement techniques, not only will you enhance your own conversational powers and meet interesting people everywhere you go, but you'll also have a positive impact on the people you encounter.

A good way to hone your acknowledgment skills is by using the "Ten-Five Rule," also known as "The Zone of Hospitality." It's an approach used by many of the world's top hotels and hospitals to make guests and patients feel welcome and acknowledged.

The rule states that if you're within ten feet of a guest or patient, make eye contact with them. If you're within five feet of them, acknowledge them by saying, "Hello." This also gives yourself the gift of being present in the moment by actively tuning into the people around you (which then makes you more approachable and easier for others to engage you).

Another acknowledgment tip is to practice on people working in the service industry, especially those who have name tags: checkout clerks, waiters, pharmacists, etc. Everyone loves hearing their own name, so give them a personal greeting you know they'll instantly appreciate.

#2 Say It Out Loud

If it still feels intimidating to break the ice with someone, start by simply sharing a random thought out loud to no one in particular. I give my client, Camden, credit for this tip …

"I've taken to just saying whatever comes into my head and it's so FREEING to just say 'you'd think a grocery store in Vancouver would have a better selection of almond butter' even if there's no one around!"

> – Camden, my client

Doing this regularly will start to carry over into your day-to-day activities when other people are around you, which presents them with the perfect opportunity to comment back to you. You'd be surprised how often it works!

#3 Do a Drive-By

"Instant joy can come from giving a compliment. The receiver and the giver both get a gift. We can get this jolt of goodness anytime we want, as often as we want… so get out there!"

> – Jennifer Blankl, dating and relationship coach

You can also do what I call a "compliment drive-by." With this approach, purposefully search for flattering aspects about the people within earshot of you, such as their beautiful earrings, colorful nail polish, or interesting tie pattern. When you see something that catches your eye, give them a genuine compliment about it and then walk away. Don't even wait for them to respond. You're outta there. Gone. See ya.

For instance, maybe you spot a woman wearing a striking shade of red lipstick. Walk up to her and say, "Your lipstick color is stunning," and then keep on walking.

This approach allows you to practice engaging with people one step at a time by removing the pressure to break the ice *and* continue the conversation in the same interaction.

Bonus: your thoughts about others will start to default to positive because you're actively looking for the good in people. More on the benefits of this in *Chapter III: Asked Out Organically*.

Besides, how often do you think a nice thought about someone yet keep it to yourself? Maybe your friend Nancy just bought you a box of chocolates for your birthday and you think, "Nancy's the best. She always makes me feel special on my birthday and remembers my favorite chocolate." When Nancy gives you the gift don't just respond with a simple, "Thank you" – tell her exactly what you were thinking about her and what she means to you.

Maybe you saw someone do a random act of kindness for another person, but the recipient didn't even acknowledge it. Go acknowledge the person who did the nice thing yourself. Even a simple, "That was very nice of you, even if that woman didn't seem to appreciate it." Since this approach has a clear purpose, it will help you become comfortable engaging with strangers, brighten someone's day, and encourage them to do another good deed for the next person.

....

Once you gain momentum doing Compliment Drive-bys,
go on a Compliment Rampage.

....

Keep up the momentum of your compliment drive-bys and turn them into a compliment rampage by setting an ambitious goal – such as dishing out five genuine compliments in the next ten minutes. Then get to it before you can overthink it.

#4 Be in Movement

Physically moving your body makes it easier to practice engaging others because it gives your nerves a natural outlet. That's another reason a "compliment drive-by" works well as a conversational warm-up: because you're in movement, not standing stationary and internalizing all that anxious energy.

If you're still feeling nervous but want to practice your chosen icebreaker approach, go to a place where people are gathered and walk around pretending to look for someone. If you're feeling extra ambitious say, "Hi!" or smile at anyone whose gaze you meet. That will get your engagement juices flowing.

#5 Phone a Friend

If you're attending an event or gathering and feeling nervous about the social aspect of it, schedule a meet-up with a friend or call a family member right beforehand to get your social skills and vocal cords warmed up.

Those familiar chats will make it easier to get into the flow of talking to people you don't know well. This is as opposed to spending all day behind a computer, having not spoken a single word out to anyone, and then trying to jump into "social mode" as soon as you step into a room full of people.

#6 Play The Rejection Game

Rejection Proof is a best-selling book about a man who went through one-hundred days of rejection. He gamified his fear in that he scored points every time he was rejected. This quickly de-sensitized him to the point that he isn't even fazed by rejection now. He also has a Rejection Therapy® game to support you on your own rejection journey.

#7 Do a Live Video

You can also gain momentum by doing live stream videos on social media. I used to be terrified of these because… well, they're live. Which means anything can happen. LIVE. But after practicing a few times and finding what works for me, now I love them because they keep me real.

It's impossible to fake your social skills when you're live; you're forced to go with the flow, even if you stumble or lose your train of thought like I still do sometimes. It's the opposite of, say, spending thirty minutes over-crafting a two-sentence text message. Which is great because you can't spend thirty minutes standing in front of someone thinking about what to say to them next; you have to think on your feet and respond in real-time. A live stream allows you to practice those spontaneous social skills from behind a screen and work up to doing the same in future face-to-face interactions.

Think about what topics you want to cover in your live stream; heck, make it into a weekly show! You might discover a hidden passion or your life's purpose in the process. Who cares if your mom and cousin Fred in Alabama are the only ones watching it? Use that small and supportive audience as a chance to hone your material, get comfortable on camera, and see what comes out of your mouth as you share your thoughts on topics you're interested in.

#8 Go to Conferences and Events

When you go to a conference or big event, you get exposed to a lot of people in a short amount of time, which makes those places perfect for finding your natural connection groove. What you don't want to do is go to one social event, try one technique on one person, and then quit. It's impossible to get into momentum; you need to try things a few times on a few different people, and then, if possible, hit-up another social gathering within 24 hours to keep up that energy.

Before heading to an event, choose a go-to question that will be relevant to everyone there, such as asking "What's your favorite part about the event so far?" Make sure it's a question you actually care to hear the answer to and then use it on as many people as you can while you're there. You'll bust through your fear in no time, which will make every single interaction after that even easier.

#9 Practice with Everyone

Gain momentum by practicing these tips with everyone as you go about your day. Carry out all your errands on the same day so you can get into social momentum by encountering lots of people in a short period of time across several different places. Moving from place to place also takes the pressure off you because you're always on your way to the next location.

Practice talking to people you aren't attracted to first, then work your way up to approaching a man who catches your eye. Try chatting-up other women and elderly men, then people in the service industry who are paid to be nice to you and don't always get treated well by those they serve. Plus – bonus! – they'll usually remember you next time and, in turn, treat you better too.

Action Items

1. Choose one of the nine actions to gain social momentum so you can get comfortable interacting with new people:

   #1 Add Some Acknowledgment

   #2 Say It Out Loud

   #3 Do a Drive-By

   #4 Be in Movement

   #5 Phone a Friend

   #6 Play The Rejection Game

   #7 Do a Live Video

   #8 Go to Conferences and Events

   #9 Practice with Everyone

2. Why did you choose that approach?

3. What action can you take to apply it within the next 48 hours?

How to Handle "One of Those Days"

Remember, being your authentic self means aligning your internal thoughts and feelings with your external words and actions.

There will be some days where you don't feel like being friendly or social and that's okay. Instead of feeling even worse by forcing yourself to practice your social skills that day, honor your emotions in that moment and take a break from engaging. If you're up for minimal interactions, try a compliment drive-by which will make you feel good without committing to a full-blown conversation.

Now you've got all The Rules of Engagement in your toolbox – whether you're approached by an enchanting stranger, or you'd like to take the reins and engage them first.

Coming Up Next...

Next up is *Chapter III: Asked Out Organically*, where I'll show you my secret approach to turn the icebreakers you discovered in *Chapter II* into a meaningful conversation and a date – as well as…

- How to set yourself apart from every other woman he's met
- How to get off boring small talk and into a meaningful conversation
- How to avoid awkward silences and always know what to say next
- How to create instant trust with someone you just met
- How to stop judging others and yourself so harshly
- How to avoid unintentionally shutting him down
- How to feel socially fulfilled regardless of your relationship status
- The instant move to stop interrupting people
- Three ways to get a date with a man you meet IRL ("in real life")
- Four ways to recover if you forget someone's name
- How to create a meaningful conversation in a group setting
- The word-for-word script of how I got a date on LinkedIn

Asked Out Organically

*Create instantly meaningful connections
and inspire a great guy to ask you out*

The secret to inspiring a great man to ask you out in the real world is to create a meaningful connection with him.

So what exactly is a "meaningful connection?" It's a genuine conversation that feels natural, not forced in any way, and gives each person a feeling of deep fulfillment.

Going even further...it's being completely present in a conversation and co-creating a shared experience. It's asking great questions – not because you're afraid of running out of things to talk about, but because you're curious about the other person and what they're sharing with you. It's letting go of judgment and being open to learning something new about yourself by listening to the experience of another person.

People are *craving* this level of connection more than ever before since our innate need for it is rarely met between all the distractions we get bombarded with every day. It's hard to achieve any level of depth when your attention is constantly being pulled in a million different directions and someone or some company always wants something from you. It feels like there's never enough time in the day, week, or year to do everything you want to do, see everyone you want to see, and go all the places you want to go.

That's part of why we tend to avoid connecting with each other when out and about; we feel like other people don't have the time and that there isn't an immediate or tangible benefit to it. So we can stay stuck on transactional small talk to get what we want or need in the moment and then go our merry way. But limiting connections to surface-level rarely - if ever - provides a feeling of fulfillment. So why do people continually stay at a superficial level?

Small talk is "safe" – but boring

Small talk serves a purpose: it's a low-risk investment to see if someone else is open to connecting further.

But when you get stuck on mundane topics for longer than a minute or two, you can get caught in The Small Talk Trap, where the conversation starts to feel incredibly draining. It can also make you feel even more lonely by limiting the connection to boring topics that neither you nor the person you're chatting with cares about.

Associating random interactions with boring conversations like this is enough to make many people want to avoid creating new connections altogether. But if they just shifted their approach slightly and discovered how to create a more fulfilling connection, it would be a completely different experience.

So if you want to create a conversation you enjoy – and get a great guy to ask you out on a date – once the other person shows they're equally invested in the chat, you'll want to get off small talk and into meaningful communication ASAP. In this chapter, I'll walk you step-by-step through how to do it.

Attraction through meaningful connection

"I've learned that people will forget what you said, people will forget what you did, but people will never forget how you made them feel."
  – Dr. Maya Angelou, poet and activist

In this chapter, you'll discover the Five Elements of a Meaningful Conversation, which is my conversational framework that gives you everything you need to create a powerful connection with anyone. Conversations will become an experience that are ten times better than any movie, TV show, or book because you're not just observing; you're living the story with another human in real-time.

This will not only feel incredibly fulfilling for you but everyone you create that connection with, which means people will naturally want more of you and the good feelings they now associate with you.

This is also moving to the next level of Maslow's Hierarchy of Needs: Self-Esteem. At this level, you're mastering the art of connecting with your fellow humans on a deep level which – surprise! – actually builds your own self-confidence and self-respect in the process. It's a beautiful cycle that can help propel you to the highest level: Self-Actualization.

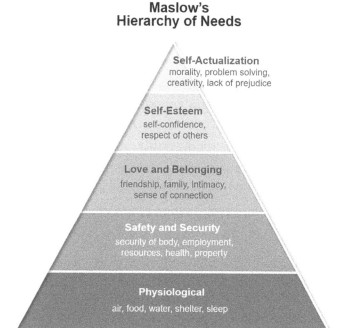

Maslow's Hierarchy of Needs

Self-Actualization
morality, problem solving,
creativity, lack of prejudice

Self-Esteem
self-confidence,
respect of others

Love and Belonging
friendship, family, intimacy,
sense of connection

Safety and Security
security of body, employment,
resources, health, property

Physiological
air, food, water, shelter, sleep

That's why the right man asking you out isn't about saying the perfect line, or wearing a hot dress, or batting your eyelashes a certain number of times. Physical attractiveness may get you noticed, but creating a meaningful connection is what gets you the date. After you've created a meaningful conversation with a man, he will naturally want more of you – and likely ask for your phone number to get it.

....

When you create a meaningful connection,
quality men naturally want more of you.

....

Once you've used the techniques in this chapter to master the art of meaningful connection, having a man ask you out is the easy part; it's simply a natural next step for him to want to see you again.

Plus, the power to create a meaningful connection isn't limited to attracting a great man; it will transform how you connect with everyone across *every* aspect of your life, just like it has for me.

Note: There are a lot of tips in this section, so remember that applying just a few of them can bring you amazing results. Find the ones that feel fun for you and fit your personality, and you'll be creating great connections with interesting people – including quality men – sooner than you think.

Results You'll Get From This Chapter

Once you master the art of meaningful connection, here are some of the results you'll enjoy…

Instant Results

★ Never endure another awkward silence again

One of the reasons people "play it safe" with meaningless chit-chat is because they aren't present in the conversation; they're either checked-out thinking about something else or already crafting a response in their head while the other person is still talking. I'll show you a simple trick to stay present in any conversation, which is also my secret to always knowing the next thing to say.

★ Every conversation becomes an energizing experience

Some self-help "experts" advise sacrificing your own enjoyment of a conversation in order to make the other person feel good. But what's the point of connecting with someone, or getting them to like you, if you can't enjoy the process too?

In *Chapter II: Effortless Engagement* I showed you how to stop draining the life out of conversations by applying The Ellen Effect, and in this chapter, I'll show you how to make conversations an energizing experience that you look forward to creating.

You'll also never get bored in a conversation again. You'll skip the vague, snooze-worthy questions like, "What's new?" and, "How are you?" and instead turn every interaction a "choose your own adventure" experience where you explore the topics that are most interesting to you.

★ Step into the position of being selective

When you have the power to give other people a great experience simply by talking to you, this puts you in the position of choosing who is worthy of your time (i.e. only the people who make *you* feel amazing too).

This natural screening process also helps you find your people; the ones who truly adore you for you. Being in this position of power completely flips any conversational fears you might have, like…

- *"Am I being annoying?"*
- *"Does he think I'm weird?"*
- *"Is he talking to me because he wants to, or is he just being polite?"*

…into an empowering reframe, such as:

- *"I'm a cool person with interesting, weird things to say – are you a cool person with interesting, weird things to say too? Let's find out!"*

★ Create a fulfilling connection with anyone

Remember Dr. Arthur Aron's study, where intimate questions led to pairs of participants falling in love with each other? In the experiment, Dr. Aron gave participants forty-five minutes to answer the questions and create a deeper connection. But I say you can create a close bond in *under a minute*. I've even brought a woman to tears within thirty seconds of meeting her!

Here's that story: I was out with a client for a "wingwoman session" where she could practice her conversation skills with me by her side for support. We were in a supermarket and as we walked by a samples table, the woman handing out food said:

"Would you like to try some hummus? It's part of my culture."

I love learning about different cultures, so I immediately homed in on that aspect and responded:

"Cool, what's your culture?"

She answered Lebanese. I asked her if the political situation at the time, in which many people from the Middle East were being denied entry into the U.S., had affected her family. She immediately took out her phone and pulled up a picture of a woman in a wedding dress. Tearing up, she told me she had missed her niece's wedding in Lebanon because she was afraid she wouldn't be able to get back into the U.S.

★ People will quickly trust and confide in you

Just like the hummus story showed, another benefit of creating a meaningful connection is that people will trust and confide in you. This builds directly off the instant rapport you learned how to create in *Chapter II: Effortless Engagement* where, by simply being your same self with everyone, people tend to trust you right off the bat. I'm privileged to have had people I just met share intimate stories with me in that first encounter, sometimes ones they hadn't even shared with their close friends or family. As you move through the Five Elements of Meaningful Conversation and keep only good intentions in mind, the people you talk to are going to sense that and trust you.

As we've previously covered, humans are *craving* this level of connection and authenticity. Every day people are flooded with an overwhelming amount of information and distractions, most with the sole motivation of hijacking their time and/or money. That means when they meet someone like you, who's able to engage them on a deeper level and sans ulterior motive, all of their unmet need for connection will likely come pouring out. So be ready, because it can happen fast.

Important note: it's an honor to have someone confide in you, so handle their share with extreme care. It can take months, or even years, to earn someone's absolute trust – and just a few seconds to lose it.

> Breaking someone's trust is like breaking a vase;
> you can piece it back together, but it will never be the same.

★ Men can't get enough of you (and ask you out to get more)

When you know how to create a meaningful connection you will instantly stand out from every other person who never goes past "safe" (i.e. boring and forgettable) topics. By applying the authentic techniques from this chapter you'll not only become instantly memorable but also a source of fascination for others.

When you give someone a taste of this intrigue, even for a few minutes, they're going to want more of it – and thus *you* – in their life. When someone wants more of something badly enough, they will find a way to get it. This includes, but is not limited to, breaking through their fear of rejection by asking you out so they can spend more time with you.

★ Filter out the wrong people (especially men) faster

Applying the Five Elements of a Meaningful Conversation creates a space of trust and sharing, which helps you quickly learn genuine aspects of the other person. Seeing someone for who they truly are helps you determine if a guy has potential to be a real match, and helps you avoid wasting time on a man who's never going to be right for you.

★ Receive powerful epiphanies + insights into your own life

"The more you are entering into the relationship of others, the more you are actually understanding yourself."
    – Esther Perel, psychotherapist and author

Creating an interesting conversation comes with the bonus of helping you learn more about *yourself* too. My guess is you don't sit around asking yourself profound questions like "What makes me truly happy?" or "What's the biggest life lesson I've learned over the past decade?"

But when you ask someone else a meaningful, open-ended question like one of those, they will almost always ask that same question back to you. And you may be surprised at what answer comes out of your mouth!

....

Articulating your thoughts in a meaningful conversation is like verbal journaling.

....

Speaking to someone in a safe space you've helped create allows you to piece together those random half-formed thoughts and questions that have been floating around in your head and turn them into concrete ideas and clear actions. Don't be surprised when, mid-conversation, you find yourself thinking something like…

"That's it! I've been trying all week to figure that out in my head. Now that I'm saying it out loud, I know the answer."

These epiphanies and moments of clarity can pop up in a conversation with anyone – from that woman you sat next to at the outdoor concert to your best friend of thirty years. You never know what insights you'll receive when answering your own interesting questions out loud to someone else.

When someone makes you feel safe enough to put those thoughts into words, you have the chance to come to your own powerful conclusions. This is exactly what I help my private coaching clients do. Only *they* truly know the answers they seek; I simply help them unlock those answers by asking the right questions that help them become conscious thoughts.

....

The answers you seek are often just one conversation away from revealing themselves to you.

....

You can also have powerful insights about yourself by simply listening to other people's experiences, stories, and moments of clarity. Even after speaking with thousands of people over the years, I continue to learn something about myself in almost every conversation. It's often easier to spot patterns and get answers when you're looking at a situation from the outside – i.e. when you don't have a personal investment in it or previous emotional attachment to it.

> Listening to someone else's story helps you see patterns and answers you may be blind to in your own life.

For example, imagine you're at an art show talking to a man who says he's taking a trip to Alaska with his friends. He then shares that he preferred to go to South Africa but was out-voted by the others, so reluctantly booked the Alaska trip.

If I was listening to this, I'd notice immediately that he decided to spend his time and money on something that he wasn't excited to do, simply so he could join his friends in what they wanted to do. My next thought would be, "I wonder what other decisions he's made in life that involved sacrificing his own desires for the sake of his friends?"

If I was in the same habit of putting my own happiness to go along with the majority, hearing his experience could be a powerful revelation for me. It's common to be blind to our own unhappy or negative patterns yet be able to instantly spot them in another person because we don't have our emotional blinders on.

You can give that man the same gift of revealing a pattern that he may be blind to. A simple question coming from a good intention such as, "That's very generous of you. Do you often do things your friends prefer over what you want to do?" He may not even realize the subconscious pattern of continually putting his happiness on hold for others until the moment you ask that.

If you want to go deeper into that topic of valuing other's preferences over his own, you could ask him a question such as:

- *"Why do you think you do that?"*
- *"How long have you been just doing whatever your friends want?"*
- *"When's the last time you did something you wanted that went against popular vote?"*

That might reveal an insecurity he also wasn't aware of ("I'm afraid I won't know how to make new friends, so I always give in to doing what mine want") or empower him to now make a different choice given the newfound clarity of this pattern he's fallen into.

> When epiphanies pop up, always capture them;
> they're going to disappear as quickly as they came.

Just like we covered in *Chapter I: Magnetic Approachability*, designate one go-to place to capture your thoughts so you free-up your attention to be present in the moment. Write them down. Email them to yourself. Capture them in OneNote, Evernote, or Panda Planner. Just put them in a place where you can give them your full attention later and stay present in the conversation at hand.

★ Enjoy the memory-boosting gift of total recall

The Empathic Listening Technique, which might be the most powerful technique I teach, is also a huge memory-booster. Applying it will help you effortlessly remember details of other people's stories, often for years or – in some of my cases – over a decade later.

This little bonus will not only impress the heck out of people, but it will also give you the Best Friend Ever Award. People appreciate being seen, heard, and acknowledged, and a great way to provide those gifts to someone is by referencing details of an important story they shared with you. Instead of just *saying* that you care about them and what's happening in their life, citing key intimate details *shows* them you do.

The secret behind the total recall phenomenon is in applying the Empathic Listening Technique, which turns a conversation into an actual experience. Just as you'd naturally remember details from an important event in your own life, you'll remember similar details when listening to other people's stories because you know how to live that story with them as they share it with you. I'll walk you step-by-step through how to use the technique, coming up.

For instance, I was catching up with my friend Mary who wanted to fill me in about a man she'd been dating long distance. I used the Empathic Listening Technique to follow along with her, noting what she said to him, how he responded, when he came to visit, what happened after that, etc. I put myself in the story with her, seeing what she saw and feeling what she felt. By the end of the story when she asked for my advice about what to do next, I could easily pull from the emotions I'd been feeling throughout her story, as well as my own personal experiences it had conjured up in the process, enabling me to be a better friend and support her on a deeper level.

What's even more interesting though is that a few weeks later, Mary and I got together with another friend and I was able to walk through her entire story again, step-by-step, to catch our other friend up on it. That's because I hadn't just blindly memorized her story; I had "lived" it on a certain level, so the details and emotions were naturally cemented in my memory. At the end of my recap, Mary said to me, "I can't believe you remembered all that. You're such a great friend!"

Lifelong Results

★ Connect with your future man on an incredibly deep level

As with many tips in this book, by discovering how to create meaningful conversations now – *before* you meet your future partner – the benefits will carry over into your relationship with him and deepen your shared bond for years to come. When you have the power to create a great conversation with someone you just met, it gives that person a preview of what life with you would be like. If it's a great experience (which it will be once I show you how to do it!), it shows them how they could spend hours, days, even years talking with you and never get bored – which is an incredibly enticing trait in a partner.

On the flip side, if you don't make it a habit to start connecting deeply with people in your life now, it's going to be even harder once you meet your match because you'll be starting from scratch. Trying to build those skills while simultaneously navigating all the other emotions and aspects of a new relationship is a lot to take on at once.

★ Avoid making painful (and expensive) life decisions

Sometimes people marry the wrong person – I get it. I've been there, done that. The same unfortunate (but valuable lesson) situation happened to one of my guy friends. Years ago, he started dating a woman who was beautiful, charming, and seemed like a real catch. He would bring her to meet-ups and holiday gatherings with our families, so I had interacted with her about a dozen times by the time he announced they were engaged.

But despite all those meet-ups, I soon realized that I'd never had anything but a surface-level conversation with her. I'd tried to ask interesting questions to get to know her better, but looking back I realized she would always give a short answer or change the topic. I had assumed that she was just a private person and saved her deep conversations for her fiancé.

Well, unfortunately, they ended up getting divorced. When I mentioned to my friend that I'd never truly connected with his ex on a meaningful level, he paused for a second and said, "You know, I don't think I ever did either."

The fact that you're reading this book means that you appreciate a deep connection and are likely interested in sharing that depth with the right man. So if you can't connect on a deeper level with him when you first meet or are getting to know him, he's outta there. A long-term commitment can't be sustained on chit-chat such as, "What park do you want to take the dog to today?" or "What movie should we see tonight?" That's why, again, it's important to start creating meaningful connections in your life right now and with *everyone* so you're all warmed-up on that front for your future relationship.

★ Feel fulfillment and find purpose by impacting others

"A colleague asked me, 'Why are you so nice to everyone? Is it tiring being like that?' and I said, 'No. When I'm nice to everyone, it makes me feel nice as well.'"

– Sajal, my client

As you've probably gathered, the benefits of creating a deep connection go well beyond having a man ask you out. You're going to be changing people's lives for the better – including your own.

Creating connections using the techniques I'll show you in this final chapter will take you from being a spectator of the world around you to an active contributor and co-creator. You'll impact people on a level of incredible depth, enable them to experience themselves in a whole new way, and give more meaning to their lives and yours.

Few people are sitting at home wondering how they can live a more meaningful life yet continue to go about their daily life feeling a sense of aimlessness and unfulfillment. The ones who do seek out a remedy for this malaise are more likely to go for a quick fix or temporary escape – like buying a new outfit or binge-watching the new season of their favorite Netflix show. But once you activate the connection superpowers I'm about to give you, it will be impossible to settle for a surface-level way of life ever again.

Here are a few examples of notes I've received after *the very first encounter* with men, thanking me for simply creating a great conversation. You'll start to get heartfelt gratitude like this from people too as you impact their lives with the connections you help create…

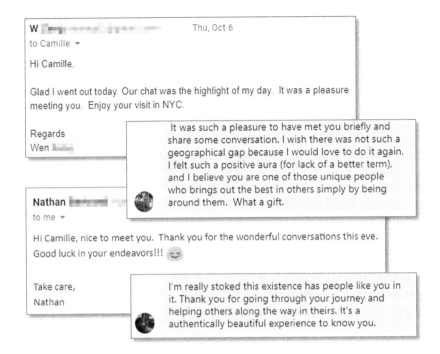

★ You'll lose that lonely feeling

"Conversation is the good stuff. It's what we crave as humans, and what provides us with the sense of community and belonging necessary to thrive."
— Cal Newport, *Digital Minimalism*

When you master the art of meaningful conversation, feelings of loneliness will start to fade away. Having these techniques in your conversational arsenal make it possible for you to connect with anybody. It's incredibly empowering to know that you're only one sentence away from feeling connected and socially fulfilled, anytime you want to be.

Warning! You'll Be a Wanted Woman

With so many people starved for meaningful connection, once you give them a taste, they'll associate those great feelings with *you*... and want more of you.

So be selective as to who continues to get your time and energy. Take a minute to reflect on who in your life right now truly lights you up and adds value, and then carve out time to cultivate deeper relationships with those people.

> Just because you make people feel good doesn't mean you give your precious time to everyone who wants it.

I'll admit it: I have an addiction to connection. I absolutely love it. But that doesn't mean I'm connecting with people 24/7. Some days I simply don't feel like being social. On those days I need to recharge my introvert batteries by being alone or go into a state of deep focus, creativity, or relaxation. I decline many social invites – from "catch-up calls," to networking events, to get-togethers – unless the invitation is from a good friend and/or there's a clear purpose for the connection that I'm equally invested in. I value a higher quality of friends versus a greater quantity because we only have so much time in our day – and in our lifetime.

How to Avoid The Catch-Up Cycle of Doom

I want you to explore every potential connection you feel inspired to create – but who you *continue* to give your time to beyond that initial interaction is a different story. Throughout each connection, pay attention to how the other person is making you feel.

Instead of setting long-term goals and aligning their life to work toward them, many people opt for short-term stimulation with activities that simply kill time and add little value – like binging reality TV, hitting the club every week, or scrolling through Instagram for hours a day.

So be aware that as someone who *is* putting in the effort to become the best version of yourself and live your best life – i.e. doing interesting things – you will be like *candy* to those short-term-focused people. In doing the hard work and continually learning about yourself, others, and the world, you'll have an endless flow of interesting stories, topics, and insights to share. This makes you extremely attractive to people who aren't living their life the same way because as you share your interesting happenings, they'll likely feel a temporary high as if *they've* enjoyed your same achievements.

But as soon as the conversation is over, that momentary escape of living vicariously through you and your cool experiences will cease to exist, and they will be anxious for the next get-together with you so they can have that same high again – without doing any of the work that you are to actually create a life like that for themselves.

This is what I call The Catch-Up Cycle of Doom. If you're not careful, you can fall into this habit of spending precious time every week "catching-up" with others who want you to regale them with tales of your adventures and discoveries… at the expense of your own goals and interests.

....

Constant "catch-up" can quickly become a major time-suck.

....

Here's an example to illustrate this situation. Imagine you have fourteen people in your life right now who want your time in some capacity. Friends, former coworkers, your college roommate, your next-door neighbor who keeps inviting you over for Scrabble, etc. They might live in your same city and ask you out for coffee or they could live on the other side of the world and want a Skype date.

So, let's say you agree to play Scrabble with your neighbor on the first of the month. The next day you meet up with a friend for a glass of wine. The next day you schedule a phone date with your cousin in Chicago. Extrapolate this out over the next two weeks where you're giving your time to a different person each day. By the end of those two weeks you will have "caught up" with fourteen people and chances are at least some will have been unfulfilling conversations such as what you've been up to, what they've been up to, and the plans each of you have coming up.

FEBRUARY 2019

Sunday	Monday	Tuesday	Wednesday	Thursday	Friday	Saturday
					1 *Person #1*	2 *Person #2*
3 *Person #3*	4 *Person #4*	5 *Person #5*	6 *Person #6*	7 *Person #7*	8 *Person #8*	9 *Person #9*
10 *Person #10*	11 *Person #11*	12 *Person #12*	13 *Person #13*	14 *Person #14*	15 *Person #1*	16 *Person #2*
17 *Person #3*	18 *Person #4*	19 *Person #5*	20 *Person #6*	21 *Person #7*	22 *Person #8*	23 *Person #9*
24 *Person #10*	25 *Person #11*	26 *Person #12*	27 *Person #13*	28 *Person #14*		

Well, guess what? By the end of those two weeks, your neighbor is going to want to get together for Scrabble *again* and hear what you've been up to the past couple weeks since he last saw you. Which means if you indulged that request – as well as all the others who will likely want the same from you – you start the fourteen-day / fourteen-person cycle all over again. Every. Two. Weeks.

> The Catch-Up Cycle of Doom means you spend more time "catching up" on the past than creating your future.

This can quickly become an endless cycle of activity-based chit-chat with many people who aren't adding equal value to your life. This will not only get boring for you *real quick* but leave you a lot less time to devote to your own self-development; an aspect which, ironically, is a big part of what they enjoy in getting together with you.

So instead of blindly accepting every invitation, you must consciously protect your time and energy. I highly recommend limiting your social life to a select handful of quality people who are creating their *own* adventures and learning new things so they also have ideas, insights, and inspirations to contribute to your conversations.

Action Items

1. How many people do you "catch up" with per month?
2. Do you come away from each of those conversations feeling energized, neutral, or drained?

All Praise and No Action Makes Anyone a Dull Boy (or Girl)

"I used to be 'that' guy who kept talking about what I was going to do. And as soon as people gave me props and validation, I wasn't as motivated to take action. As a result, I got caught up with trying to 'look' successful rather than actually trying to 'be' successful. I realized that it's much more motivating to talk about what I've already done rather than what I'm going to do."

— Myke Macapinlac, dating expert

Studies have shown that when a person shares their goals and achievements it gives them a feeling of accomplishment... even when they haven't taken any action toward achieving it yet.

This enables people to reap rewards – such as praise and admiration from others – without actually earning it. Left unchecked, some people fall into the trap of making this their new normal – i.e. all talk, no walk. Hence the guy whose go-to party conversation topic is always how he's "working on his novel," yet he hasn't written anything in years.

People who are action-takers will catch on to this quickly and usually try to distance themselves for fear the "all talk, no walk" habits of the other person will rub off on them. At least that's how I feel. It's taken me a long time to build productive habits, so I want to surround myself with people who reinforce my drive to take action, not discourage it.

The Five Elements of a Meaningful Conversation

"Be brave enough to start a conversation that matters."
    – Jonathon Aslay, conscious dating expert

Using the Five Elements gives every conversation a purpose and a direction, which means no more pointless, "where the hell is this going?" interactions for you.

The framework creates a structure that naturally guides every chat into interesting topics, far better than any dialogue you could force or pre-plan in your head. I recommend applying the Five Elements to every single conversation you have, so they simply become a natural habit that you don't even have to consciously think about doing.

....

Each conversation may vary by topic and person,
but the five key elements will always be the same.

....

But enough teasers – here are the Five Elements of a Meaningful Conversation:

1) Ask Awesome Questions
2) Hold Space for Silence
3) Listen Like Your Life Depends Upon It
4) Release Judgment
5) Share Insights and Stories

Recap: The Four-Word Transition to Meaningful

Before we dive into each Element, here's where we left off in the previous chapter, which was all about how to break the ice with someone. Because at some point that initial topic will die (usually indicated by the fact that you're not enjoying it anymore). Once that happens, it's time to transition to a meaningful level and the quickest way to do that is by asking a personal question, like:

- *"How's your day going?"*
- *"Where are you headed?"*
- *"Good event so far?"*

This is how you can tell if that handsome stranger complimented your yellow suede jacket because he genuinely liked it, or because he was using it as a reason to talk to you. A simple question, like the examples above, enables the other person to answer with as much or as little information as they want, which will instantly reveal whether they're interested in continuing the conversation or not.

Your Biggest Fears Are Your Biggest Opportunities

Your biggest fears around talking to other people are actually your best opportunities to create a deeper connection. Once you discover how to reframe your fears into these opportunities, you'll have mastered the art of meaningful connection. I'll show you how, coming up.

❀ Element 1: Ask Awesome Questions

"Every man I meet is my superior in some way. In that, I learn of him."
    – Ralph Waldo Emerson, American poet

- <u>Fear</u>: *"What if I have nothing in common with this person?"*
- <u>Symptom</u>: Avoidance of talking to strangers.
- <u>Reframe</u>: *Nothing* in common = *everything* to learn about!
- <u>Remedy</u>: The Art of Asking Awesome Questions.

Worried you can't find anything in common with that hilarious guy you met at the bowling alley? Having little to nothing in common with someone can make for a great conversation. Here's a powerful reframe for that fear:

> Reframe: Having *nothing* in common with someone means
> I have *everything* to ask about them.

Think about a recent movie you've seen or book you've read. Odds are you chose it to learn more about the subject, right? If you already knew every tiny detail about the topic or the story, you wouldn't have wasted your time on it. You invested in it because you had some level of interest in learning something new, even if it was a subject you were already familiar with.

The same goes for conversations. As humans, we all have a few essential aspects in common – like the need to eat, sleep, and fund our lifestyle. So if you're scrambling for a topic to talk about, start with those. Here are some example questions:

- *"Where are you from?"*
- *"What was it like growing up there?"*
- *"What brought you to [current city]?"*
- *"What do you do for fun?"*

- *"Do you enjoy cooking?"*
- *"What's your favorite restaurant in town?"*
- *"Why is it your favorite?"*
- *"How did you discover it?"*
- *"Describe the best meal you had there."*
- *"What do you do for work?"* (I'll show you an easy way to make the "work" topic more personal and interesting later in the chapter)

As you ask, keep an eye out for natural tangents that lead into other topics you're interested in so that you can learn something new and/or go even deeper. Maybe the other person answers the question, "What brought you to [current city]" by describing how she went from her hometown in the Upper Peninsula of Michigan to Santa Fe, New Mexico, followed by a year abroad in Singapore, and is now settled in San Francisco. Now those are stories I want to hear more about, which means I'd have plenty of questions about each of those places.

> The best questions to ask are unconventional,
> thought-provoking, and fun to answer.

Asking questions is also a great way to calm your nerves by turning the conversation spotlight away from you and onto the other person for a while. Like we covered earlier, it also gives the gift of self-reflection to someone who otherwise may have never come to those powerful, potentially life-changing conclusions on their own. Just be prepared to have those same questions asked back to you too.

Say It Like You Mean It

When you have only a good intention (versus one stemming from judgment), you can ask anyone almost any question. The key is that it must come from a place of pure curiosity and compassion because people can almost always feel the real meaning behind spoken words.

The same rule applies when you're answering someone else's question. I used to struggle with giving my honest opinion to someone when they asked for it because sometimes I knew it wasn't what they were hoping to hear. But skipping the truth for the sake of "sparing" someone's feelings is only being kind to *yourself* by avoiding making yourself feel uncomfortable. If someone asks for your opinion, ask them if they want the truth. If they say yes, kindly give it to them. Keyword: *kindly*.

For example, one of your girlfriends tells you about her recent breakup and asks for your advice on what to do about it. You already know that her ex is pretty much the same type of man as her last three. Clearly, she can't see her pattern of choosing the wrong men and thus continues to make the same mistakes. If you truly wanted the best for her, you'd push past the potential awkwardness in revealing your insight into the situation. By avoiding telling her the truth to "spare her feelings" she may remain blind to it, which basically dooms her to keep repeating it. That's not being a good friend to her.

You can point it out directly with an intention of kindness:

- *"I care about you and here's what I'm seeing as a pattern, what do you think?"*

Or indirectly using questions that help lead her to her own realization:

- *"What advice would you give me if I were you in this situation?"*
- *"Did you think about it this way?"*
- *"Did he ever treat you well?"*

It's all about how you say it – your tone, your phrasing, and most of all your intention. Asking a question with genuine concern is completely different than asking it with the intention to judge someone with the goal of making yourself feel better.

Fact: people rarely introduce topics that they don't want to talk about. So if the person you're chatting with brings up a seemingly sensitive story or subject, it's fair game for you to ask more questions. In fact, I bet they *want* you to ask about it because everyone else they tried to talk to about it had avoided inquiring further about it; ironically for fear of being rude.

....

When someone brings up a sensitive topic,
that's usually their subtle invitation to talk more about it.

....

Be Authentically Curious

"When an old man dies, a library burns to the ground."
   – African Proverb

You can learn something new from everyone you meet, so approach each person with genuine curiosity and an inquisitive mindset, such as…

- *"I wonder what her story is…"*
- *"What's the one thing he's really excited about right now?"*
- *"What keeps her up at night?"*
- *"What can I learn about myself from him?"*
- *"Could she be a new friend or maybe introduce me to my future husband? Let's find out!"*

Even if you've known the other person forever, you *definitely* don't know everything about them. You can spend a lifetime trying to learn all the different aspects of yourself and still barely scratch the surface.

Besides, life is constantly changing for each of us. Maybe you've known a friend for ten years, but in the past six months, he's started his own business or won a battle against cancer. He's going to be a slightly different person after going through a big life change like those, or at least now has different insights and stories to share than he did prior to them.

The key to asking great questions is to only ask ones you want to know the answers to; i.e. that you care about on some level. Asking boring questions that neither you nor the other person cares about is a fast way to make yourself, and them, mentally check-out of the conversation.

....
If a question isn't fun for you to ask,
it probably isn't fun for someone to answer.
....

Ask Questions You Want Asked Back to You

If it's hard to muster up curiosity or affection for someone you've only known for a few minutes, ask a great question for the sole purpose of discovering more about *yourself*.

....
You can learn something new about yourself
in every conversation you have.
....

Imagine you're in line at the art supplies store and run into your elderly neighbor George. You've chatted with George on and off over the years and thought you knew all that you needed to know about him: retired naval officer, widower, no kids, loves baseball.

But after spotting a chisel in George's shopping cart and asking about it, you discover he used to be a well-known sculptor in Paris. What?! How did George make the transition from naval officer to high-profile sculptor – and what can you learn about your own career path from his experiences?

A few examples of questions that may come to you in that moment:

- *"How did you find your talent for sculpting?"*
- *"What was the transition from armed forces to artist like?"*
- *"How did your life change when you made that transition?"*
- *"What was your biggest fear in doing it?"*
- *"What was the biggest lesson you learned from it?"*
- *"Any advice for someone who wants to jump into a different career?"*

Ask yourself what you can learn from others' experiences and questions like these will naturally start popping in your head. Then let people surprise you! Not only will you get a hit of inspiration about your own life choices and options, but you'll make the day of the other person who now gets to share a part of their life with you. It's a beautiful win-win.

Also, chances are that George will pick up from your questions that you're considering a career change and ask you insightful questions about that, which will help you articulate all those half-formed thoughts and mixed feelings that you've been trying to process on your own until now.

By the way, elderly people have *the best stories*. Talk to them, ask them questions, and learn from them. They are a wealth of information and life lessons. They also, sadly, have one of the highest rates of loneliness, so giving them the gift of connection – even if just for a moment – can have an incredible impact.

Asking questions about topics that you're interested in is also a "hack" to steer the conversation toward your favorite topics, which then sets up the conversation to naturally showcase your awesome personality and life (more on how to do this coming up in Element 5).

Go for Depth, Not Breadth

The fastest way to turn a conversation into an interview is by constantly switching topics, which prevents going deeper into any one of them.

For example, I had a dinner date with a man who played a not-so-fun game of 20 Questions. It was almost as if he had a set of "Completely Unrelated Questions to Ask on a Date" and was simply going down the list. He would ask one and I would answer, but when I tried to ask it back to him, he was already onto the next random question which had nothing to do with the previous one. We ran out of things to talk about in about ten minutes and our food hadn't even arrived yet. On the flip side, if we had gone deeper on any one of those questions, we could have talked about it for hours.

So instead of jumping around, find a topic you're genuinely interested in and ask insightful questions about it until it naturally segues to another interesting topic. To go deeper on a specific topic, ask questions related to how someone thinks or feels, or the "why" behind what they did.

Examples of feeling, thinking, and "why" questions:

- *"How do you feel about that?"*
- *"Why did you do that?"*
- *"What made you say that?"*
- *"What was running through your head?"*
- *"Tell me more!"*

As you go deeper, be prepared to find out fascinating things you never knew or could have guessed about the other person. Heck, they'll find out fascinating things about *themselves* they never knew, because they haven't been asking themselves thought-provoking questions like that.

If you tend to make flash judgments about others, getting to a level of depth like this can help dispel those quick – and often incorrect – assessments. Maybe you thought your balding, middle-aged coworker in the next cubical was a boring man with no social life outside of his cat. Until one morning you run into him in the office kitchen and ask how his weekend was…only to discover that he used to be a world-class chess player…or grew up in the highlands of Sri Lanka…or enjoys dressing up as Sailor Moon at Comic-Con events.

Get curious about who people *really* are and be open to going beyond your initial perceptions of them. Every one of us is a complex creature who experiences thousands of different thoughts and emotions every day – as well as our own dreams, fears, regrets, traumas, and joys that have spanned decades of our existence.

....

Make it your mission to learn something from each person, because there is *always* something interesting to discover.

....

List: Best Types of Questions

All relationships start with one conversation – so make each one a good one and you might find a lifelong friend or partner in the process.

In summary, here's a cheat sheet of great types of questions that can lead to a meaningful conversation:

- Ask open-ended questions related to feelings, thoughts, advice, and opinions.
  - (see previous examples in "Go for Depth Not Breadth")
- Add details to your open-ended questions.
  - The more specific the question, often the easier and more fun it is to answer.
- Turn a question around on the other person.
  - Instead of answering the question *"What do you do for work?"*
  - Playfully ask back *"What do you think I do for work?"*
- Ask a hypothetical question that's *actually possible* (e.g. not *"Would you rather smell like cotton candy or hot chocolate for the rest of your life?"* – I hate those pointless questions).
  - *"If you could do anything without failing, what would you do?"*
  - *"If you could master any skill, what would it be?"*
  - *"If you could have another home in any place in the world, where would it be?"*
- Go for depth of questions, not breadth.
- Ask questions that you truly care about.
- Ask questions that you want asked back to you.
  - You can learn a lot about *yourself* in conversations with others.
- Bring up topics that interest you or you want to go deeper on.

Action Items

1. List five topics/aspects about others that you're curious about.
2. How can you turn each of those into a question to ask them?

⟡ Element 2: Hold Space for Silence

"Silence is one of the great arts of conversation."
– Cicero, Roman philosopher

- <u>Fear</u>: *"What if we hit an awkward silence?"*
- <u>Symptom</u>: Constantly filling the natural silence with forced and/or superficial topics.
- <u>Reframe</u>: The longer the silence, the more meaningful and interesting the answer might be.
- <u>Remedy</u>: Allow as much time and space as needed for yourself or the other person to answer.

If you have a fear of hitting an awkward silence, you may find yourself jumping in to fill every potential pause to prevent an uncomfortable moment. But here's the irony: constantly cutting the silence (or people) off like this reduces the quality of the conversation which leads to even more painful silences.

It makes the other person feel like you don't care about their answer, which usually makes them want to stay within the safety of small talk… which then leads to more frequent moments of dead air because no one knows – or cares about – where to take the conversation.

> Hold the space for the other person to answer with as much or as little information as they want to.

Remember, all silences are not created equal. If you're in a bar or club and the music suddenly stops, everyone knows that means it's time to leave. But silence or a long pause in the middle of a conversation can mean you inspired an insightful response that the other person simply needs a few extra seconds to think about. Or perhaps it's simply giving space for the next topic of the conversation to naturally reveal itself to both of you.

As you become comfortable holding space for silence, it shows the other person that you're comfortable with yourself and with them in that you don't need to force or prove anything in that moment. It also shows that you value hearing their response and are confident enough to hold the space for them to process and share it, which creates a safe place for them to open up even more.

Reframe: the longer the silence, the more meaningful and interesting the answer may be.

The way to overcome your fear of awkward silences is the same as getting comfortable with eye contact. Gradually push your comfort level with it, by a fraction of a second each time. This will start to build trust with yourself that you won't die when you hit a natural pause with someone. It also hones your ability to determine when a silence is, "I'm still thinking" or "It's your turn to say something / Let's change topics."

Remember: *both* people in the conversation are responsible for holding space for the silence. It's not solely your responsibility to handle it – although now you know exactly how to do it.

Element 3: Listen Like Your Life Depends Upon It

"By really hearing a man, you make him feel special and cared for in a very powerful way… If you really want to make every man want you, become a masterful listener."

– Marie Forleo, *Make Every Man Want You*

- <u>Fear</u>: *"What if I run out of things to say or don't know what to say next?"*
- <u>Symptom</u>: Crafting your response while the other person is still talking.
- <u>Reframe</u>: Staying present in the conversation is the key to *always* knowing what to say next.
- <u>Remedy</u>: Presence + Acknowledgment = Great Conversation (i.e. your *presence* is a *present*)

In this section, I'll show you my secret way to stay engaged and interested in any conversation and how to make it into a sensory experience. I'll also show you how to give the gift of acknowledgment and appreciation, which inspires others to return that incredible gift back to you.

But first, let's tackle the symptom that comes with the fear of not knowing what to say next: formulating your response while the other person is still talking. The irony here is that when you stop listening to someone in favor of crafting your response to them, it prevents the one action that enables you to always keep the conversation going: listening. Truly listening to the other person means you're following along with their story, which inherently provides clues about what the next question, topic, or comment might be.

Reframe: Giving a conversation my full attention
always provides me with what to say next.

In this section, we'll cover three aspects of how to be a great listener:

- The Empathic Listening Technique
- Acknowledge Without Interrupting
- Loosen Your Grip

The Empathic Listening Technique

The Empathic Listening Technique ("ELT") gives you the power to harness the #1 key to creating a meaningful conversation…

> The #1 key to creating meaningful conversation
> is to *listen in images*.

Visual listening is a technique I'd been unknowingly practicing for years, completely unaware until I casually described the process to a client in a coaching session a few years ago. Her response of "That's amazing!" made me realize it might not be something other people were naturally doing. It was also the perfect example of an epiphany that was only able to come to me via creating a meaningful conversation. Otherwise, I would have continued to assume everyone else was a visual listener too.

I'll walk you step-by-step through the process of listening in images, which is simply immersing yourself in the story of the speaker by putting yourself in their place as they describe what's happening. When you do this, every conversation will become *an experience*.

- You'll see what they see
- You'll feel what they feel
- You'll be experiencing their story as if you were them

> Visualizing the other person's story naturally keeps you
> present and focused on the conversation.

It's Like Adult Storytime – But Better

Humans are inherently wired to love stories. It's how our ancestors passed down crucial life lessons from one generation to the next, long before we invented writing. This means when you hear someone launch into the start of a story, Mother Nature has programmed you to pay attention.

Using the Empathic Listening Technique is like going back to the storytime readings of your childhood. Imagine your eight-year-old self, sitting on the floor of your classroom gathered around your teacher as she read a book out loud. What were you doing as you listened to it?

Were you worried about cleaning your room? Or what you were having for dinner? Or whether you should get together with Laura or Tanya that weekend?

Of course not.

You were fully present and completely captivated by the story that was unfolding before you, getting lost in the magical setting, imagining each mythical character, and feeling the emotions of the adventure. You were visually following along, carried away in the enjoyment of a spellbinding story.

Somewhere between your eight-year-old self (who was able to create a sensory experience from a simple narrative) and yourself of today (an adult living amongst endless distractions and obligations) you've likely forgotten how to tap into that visual listening process that once came to you as second nature.

But, great news: I'm about to return that power to you right now.

The best part? The stories you hear, the experiences you create from them, and the emotions you feel in the process are going to be even *better* than storytime of your childhood because they're about real life, real people, and real emotions.

Plus, if something didn't make sense to you in a book, show, or movie, you couldn't ask the characters for additional context, or go deeper on how they're feeling about it. In a conversation "story," you now have that power. No plot holes or questions need to go unanswered.

How to create on-demand experiences

As soon someone else starts sharing, put on your visual listening cap and drop yourself into their shoes to become part of their story. See what they see and feel what they feel as if you were them in that moment.

Here's an example: you're at a networking event talking to a man who's sharing about a stressful work meeting he had that afternoon. Immediately put yourself in a meeting room. Imagine you're feeling anxious. Maybe even recall an actual work meeting from your own past where you were stressed out – or picture one of your past managers who was a little intimidating. Start to paint the picture of where he was and what he was going through as he describes it. Then feel those same emotions.

To stay in someone's story, you'll likely need more information than what they initially provide you with. Since it's their story, they're already familiar with all the details and might gloss over or leave out some crucial bits that help paint the full picture for someone who wasn't there. You can get any missing context by asking questions about the setting, characters, and emotions involved. This also shows the person that you're truly listening to their story and want to know more about it:

- *"Why were you there?"*
- *"How do you know that person?"*
- *"Why did you say it that way?"*

Asking clarifying questions transforms someone's old story
into a new experience for both of you.

These questions aren't random, they serve a specific purpose: to give you enough information about the story so you can insert yourself into it:

- Environment (what's the setting?)
- Encounters (who's there and what interactions are going on?)
- Emotions (what are you feeling and why?)

Asking these questions gives the information you need to follow along in the story. The more details you receive about the story, the more questions will naturally pop-up and provide endless interesting topics to talk about.

It's the same phenomenon that happens when you stalk someone on social media: the more information you get, the more you want. Never ask questions simply for the sake of filling space. Make sure you're invested in each question and it's directly relevant to keeping you visually and emotionally connected to the other person's story.

Go deeper on topics that interest you

The Empathic Listening Technique enables you to expand on the topics that interest you the most. If you love to travel, ask questions about the setting, the people, and the culture. If you're a foodie, ask about the meals involved. Personally, I try to steer conversations toward the topic of interpersonal relationships so I can learn more about the other person in the context of those. Asking questions around your personal interests also allows you to pull in your own memories around those same topics, which starts merging your life experiences with the other person's story.

> Applying the Empathic Listening Technique gives you
> the power to go from "listener" to "experiencer."

It's like making every conversation a "chose your own adventure," where you help guide the story and add to it. More on how you can comfortably contribute to it, coming up. This is also when powerful clarity and epiphanies in your own life tend to happen: when you're looking at your own experiences through the lens of someone else's story.

The only time you should ever interrupt someone is when asking for more information about *their* story. If you're a perpetual interrupter (or want to know how to handle one), I'll reveal why people interrupt the next section, "How to Acknowledge Without Interrupting" – as well as the instant fix for it so your conversations will flow ten times better.

ELT Example #1: Hiking Mount Everest

Here's an example of the Empathic Listening Technique in action. Imagine you're at a party talking to a cute guy you just met:

You: *"So what's a personal highlight from the past six months?"*

- You had this question prepped before the party, but now that you've asked it, it's time to stop pre-planning and simply be present in the moment.

Him: *"I just got back from hiking Mount Everest. It was life-changing."*

- He gave you a setting: Mount Everest. So picture yourself on a huge mountain.
- Now, what's it look like? Blue skies, you're up in the clouds, not a lot of people around.
- What's it feel like? Freaking COLD.
- But you need more information in order to keep visualizing yourself in his story...
  - Why are you on Everest?
  - How did you get there?
  - How are you feeling now that you're standing there?
  - Did you have to prepare or train for the hike?
- Pick one of those questions (or come up with your own) that you want to dive deeper into.

You: *"That's incredible! What made you want to hike Everest?"*
Him: *"Two years ago I took an Uber and my driver was a Sherpa who had summited the mountain twice. He had amazing things to say about it and I just knew I had to do it."*

- Ok, a new situation has now been introduced. This is where the "choose your own adventure" part comes in...
- Depending on which scene feels the most interesting, you can either...
    1. Picture yourself sitting in an Uber with a Nepalese Sherpa and follow up with more questions about that moment. OR
    2. Go back to the Everest setting and ask more questions to play out that experience instead.
- Let's say you chose Everest. You already have the setting and now know why you're there. So what do you need to know or care about next to continue the story? Putting yourself in his shoes, you might be wondering...
    • Do you have a friend there – or did you go alone?
    • How big is your hiking group?
    • How many days did it take?
    • Just how cold *was* it?
- Note: These are probably the last clarifying questions you need in order to paint enough of a picture and "get into the role" of the storyteller. After you have enough information to visually insert yourself in the environment and logistics of the event, it's time to ask deeper questions about his experience and the thoughts and emotions behind it.

You: *"Did you go with a friend or alone?"*

Him: *"I went by myself. Our hiking group was small, with people from all over the world – me from the US, a couple from India, a man from Egypt, and three women from Australia."*

- Immediate first thought: This man is a confident risk-taker who's comfortable going on adventures alone and taking action on his dreams.
    • Next thought: Wonder what other great stories he has.
    • Next thought: He went alone, which might mean he's single... hmmm.

- Before pivoting to those tangents, I'd personally want to go deeper on this Everest experience. Because hello, life-changer!
- Remember: go for depth of questions, not breadth. Asking surface-level questions which aren't vital to the story at this point can wait.

You: *"What an eclectic group. Ok, tell me about the hike – how was that experience?"*

- This is a purposefully open-ended question that gives him the space to share his most memorable anecdote.
  - That means he'll love sharing it (who doesn't love telling their best story to someone genuinely interested in hearing it?)
  - That also means you're about to hear an entertaining story about a hike on Mount Everest directly from the man who experienced it. Yes, please!
- As he's talking, listen for other aspects you want to go deeper on.

Him: *"It was even harder than I thought it'd be. Definitely the most challenging thing I've ever done in my life. Both physically and mentally."*

- Sharing that it was the most challenging thing he's ever done is his invitation to go deeper. At that point, most people listening would say something like "I bet it was." and leave it at that. But not you.
- He just gave you two topics to go even deeper into: the physical challenges and the mental challenges.
  - If you're into sports or fitness you might choose to ask questions about the physical aspect.
  - Personally, I love emotions, so I'd ask about the mental aspect.

You: *"Interesting. Tell me more about the mental challenges."*

- This creates a safe space for him to go deeper by telling him you want to know more, then turning it back to him to answer with as much or as little information as he wants to provide.
- You can bet he wasn't hiking Everest, braving the brutal elements for a couple weeks, staying on surface-level thoughts. He probably

had some profound perspective changes; which I know I'd love to hear more about. Whether he's willing to share those deeper thoughts is up to him, but at least you've done everything you could to inspire him to go there.

I could continue this example forever, but hopefully, this paints enough of a conversational picture to show you how the Empathic Listening Technique can be used in this conversation.

ELT Example #2: A friend's lunch date debrief

You don't have to encounter the next Sir Edmund Hillary to use the Empathic Listening Technique or create a meaningful conversation. Here's an example of how to use it with a friend who just came back from a lunch she wants to tell you about:

Her: *"I just came from a great lunch."*
You: *"Cool, where'd you go?"*

- Try to get the setting first so you can start painting the picture and insert yourself into it.

Her: *"I met a friend at Noelle, that restaurant near the university."*

- You have a setting – but who's the friend? You need a face or a feeling of who this person is.

You: *"Which friend?"*
Her: *"Mika, my friend from college, you met her last month."*

- Now you've got a visual of place and person. Perfect.
- Time to jump to an open-ended question and let her tell the story in her own way about why the lunch was so special.

You: *"Oh yeah, she's awesome! What made lunch so great?"*

- Your only job now is to listen intently and watch for topics you want to go deeper into.

Her: *"She just tried this new acrobatic class – I didn't know we had those in Kansas City. She invited me to go next week. I'm a little nervous though."*

- Sharing that she's nervous is your invitation to ask why.

You: *"Sounds fun. What makes you nervous about it?"*
Her: *"Hmmm. Well…I think I'm scared of trying new things. It's been a while since I did anything outside my usual routine."*

- Your question is helping her process her own fear. She was aware that she felt nervous, but not *why*.
- This is now also bringing up a similar question for yourself: when was the last time *you* did something outside your comfort zone?

You: *"What makes going outside your routine so scary?"*

- You're going deeper, but not in an intrusive or uncomfortable way. It's the natural next question that she clearly hasn't thought about but would probably enjoy answering and benefit from.

Her: *"I'm afraid I'll realize how out of shape I am. And that I'll look like an idiot compared to everyone else who's been taking the class for weeks."*

- Ah, fear of judgment from others.
- Now think about your own situation and the last time you pushed outside your comfort zone. She's shared her story, now feel free to chime in and relate to her with one of your own experiences that's similar. I'll show you exactly how to do it in Element Five, coming up.

The Empathic Listening Technique is doable (I promise)

"Becoming consciously aware of the way we behave, and why, is an epiphany. As with learning a language, we can memorize all we wish – but it's only in applying what we've studied that the pieces are made whole."
    – Jeff, my insightful multilingual cousin

If those two examples of the ELT process feel overwhelming, please believe me that after a little practice and finding your own rhythm with it, it can become almost second nature.

Start with simply visualizing the story setting and feeling the emotions that go with it. After a while it will become a habit you fall into every time someone starts talking to you. Which means you won't be expending energy because it's simply your natural default – you won't even notice you're doing it, but your conversations become one-hundred times more interesting and fun.

Remember, I was doing this process subconsciously for two decades without even realizing it. That's how natural it can become when you keep practicing and discover the approach, questions, etc. that feel best for you. You'll know you've found your groove when conversations start feeling exciting instead of draining.

Action Items

1. Describe how well you listen to a friend who's speaking.
2. Describe how well you listen to someone you don't know well or just met when they're speaking.
3. How can you apply the Empathic Listening Technique to become a better listener across all conversations?

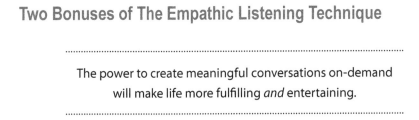

Two Bonuses of The Empathic Listening Technique

The power to create meaningful conversations on-demand
will make life more fulfilling *and* entertaining.

Bonus #1: This new approach to conversations will feel like you're adding experiences to *your* life. Just like a good movie or book, you can come away from a conversation feeling as if you lived the experience yourself. I remember one time I used the ELT as my friend was describing her trip to the beaches of Curaçao. By the end of the story, I honestly felt like I'd just gone on a mini-vacation!

Yet another reason to surround yourself with action-takers:
interesting people have interesting stories.

Bonus #2: I guarantee the vast majority of people in the world do not give this level of attention to other people's stories, which makes you an instant rarity in their eyes when you do. It also makes them feel appreciated on a level they likely haven't felt in a long time, if ever. That means they're going to associate those feelings of fulfillment directly with you and will probably want more of you – a lot more. So if they ask for more of your time, either in the moment or in following up with you later, remember to make sure they are someone you enjoy and want to invest more time in too.

Disclaimer: Watch out for these topics

If you're sensitive to violence and/or graphic topics, stop visualizing those aspects as soon as they enter the story. I had to learn this the hard way after a few unpleasant instances.

One time was when I was sixteen and listening to a family friend share way too much detail about her recent heart surgery. As a teenager with no clue what "visual listening" was, I subconsciously launched into my natural process of listening in images, which meant I was visualizing her heart blockage inside of my own body suddenly breaking free and traveling through me… well, I don't want to relive it. Anyway, I remember feeling light-headed, then waking up on the ground after a full-on faint.

Over the years, it took a few more times of physically passing out from visualizing graphic stories to realize that I just can't handle them. Although, for whatever reason, that fact has not prevented my love for *Game of Thrones*.

If you're a sensitive or empathic person, or just don't do well with violence or gore, speak up as soon you hear one of those topics introduced into the conversation and ask the speaker to either keep them vague or change to another topic.

Side Note: we're getting deep into the Five Elements, so just a reminder you can see a visual of how all these sections flow together in the *Guide: All Book Sections by Page Number* on page 237.

Acknowledge Without Interrupting

When I'm sharing a story, idea, insight, or even just stream of consciousness trying to process something out loud to someone I trust, even one word from the other person can break my flow and make me forget what I was talking about.

Also, nothing says, "I don't care about what you're saying, can we talk about me now?" faster than interrupting someone. Interrupting not only risks losing your train of thought but will likely keep both parties stuck on surface-level topics because there's been no safe space to feel truly seen or heard.

Here's why people interrupt

If you're a chronic interrupter, or know someone who is, take a look at these five reasons for interrupting and see which one you (or they might) identify with most to understand the deeper "why" – and how to stop:

#1 You want to show you're listening

Ironically, interrupting someone to show that you're listening (even a simple "OMG that sounds so scary!") only accomplishes the opposite. It breaks the flow of the other person's thoughts and makes them feel like you're not listening.

#2 You get genuinely excited and inspired to contribute

I know, I know. Sometimes we all get excited or have a breakthrough we want to immediately share. But think about how you feel when you're in the middle of a sentence and someone is continually interrupting you with their own insights. It's annoying as hell and can make you question if it's worth continuing the conversation because you feel like they're more focused on when they get to speak.

#3 You want to share your insight before you forget it

I understand this too. I tend to lose a thought as quickly as it appears if I don't immediately note it somewhere. The Empathic Listening Technique will help with this. By visualizing and feeling the emotions of someone else's story, it's easier to recall what inspired your idea or epiphany because you can simply retrace your steps in the story. So take heart that you can likely recapture your idea and wait until the other person is done talking to share it with them.

If you're *really* worried that you'll forget your brilliant insight, whip out your phone or a notepad and jot it down so you can reference it once the other person has finished. Yep, doing this is *less* disruptive than verbally interrupting the other person to share your thought in the moment. As you type or write out the thought, say to them, "Keeping talking, you just inspired a thought," which will give them permission to keep going while allowing you to capture the thought. Plus, you just created an instantly sexy "teaser" since they're going to want to know what they inspired for you. Boom!

#4 You think you know what they're going to say

Personally, this one drives me *nuts*. Assuming that you know what someone else is going to say is condescending, even if unintentionally so. There's a difference between jumping in to help someone put words to a thought they're struggling to express, versus cutting someone off before they're done. The latter essentially says to them, "I think I know where this might be going; but even if I'm wrong, I don't care because I want to say it." Rude!

#5 You want to turn the topic back to you

Last reason for interrupting: you didn't know you were doing it or weren't aware of the effect it was having on others. Good news: awareness is the first step to recovery, so now that it's out in the open, ask yourself why you've been doing it. Think of a time when you interrupted someone – what were you needing in that moment? Appreciation, attention, validation? Sit with it for a bit.

> The fastest way to get appreciation, attention, and validation is by first giving it to someone else.

When you start genuinely giving what you need to other people, it will start coming back to you in spades.

Going even deeper: relying on external validation from others is a battle you will never win; *you* are the only one who can ever provide the validation and appreciation you're seeking. So think of what you need from others and then find a way to give that to yourself – be it validation, acceptance, admiration, or unconditional love.

Action Items

1. Do you have a habit of interrupting people?
2. If so, what's the deeper reason you're doing it?

    #1 You want to show you're listening

    #2 You get genuinely excited and inspired to contribute

    #3 You want to share your insight before you forget it

    #4 You think you know what they're going to say

    #5 You want to turn the topic back to you

    • Another reason?

The Interruption Remedy

Now that we've covered the root causes behind interrupting, here's what you do about it...

If you're the cut-off culprit

Meaningful connection means no interruptions – unless you're jumping in to ask a clarifying question to stay in the other person's story. The fastest and easiest way to stop the habit of interrupting while still showing that you're listening is by making eye contact, nodding your head, and channeling anything you want to say into "Mmmms" and "Hmmms."

Since those aren't actual words and are expressed with a closed mouth, they show that you're following along without breaking the speaker's flow.

Dealing with a serial interrupter

If someone keeps interrupting you, assume they're doing it for one of the well-intentioned reasons mentioned earlier and lovingly call it out.

Here are a few methods to try…

- Hold up one finger to signal, *"I'm not done yet."*
- Say, *"Please let me finish"* and then smile
- Say, *"I know you don't mean to be rude, but you keep interrupting."*

Loosen Your Grip

Someone once asked me, "What's one area of your life you purposefully don't plan?" My immediate answer was, "Conversations."

I love feeling in control of most aspects of my life – from who I spend my time with, to what I want to eat for dinner to which hotel I book for vacation. I used to apply that same need for control to my conversations, probably because I had an intense fear of awkward silences – as well as a fear of appearing boring. Over time I realized that my best conversations happened when I stopped pre-planning what to say and simply surrendered to the natural flow.

> Trying to force a conversation is exactly what's making
> your worst conversation fears come true.

I now enter every conversation with the same excitement as a new adventure, because I honestly have no idea where it will go which can be quite thrilling. I do know it will naturally flow better places than anywhere I could ever pre-plan, and I've proven that truth to myself thousands of times.

> You can start a conversation with a pre-planned question –
> but then release control and just be present.

⚛ Element 4: Release Judgment

"…when I can open up and see another person in a fresh way, my own self-image transforms."

   – Susan Gillis Chapman, *The Five Keys of Mindful Communication*

- <u>Fear</u>: *"I don't want to come off as rude or intrusive."*
- <u>Symptom</u>: Stuck on surface level questions and topics.
- <u>Reframe</u>: Releasing judgment about someone allows me to show a genuine interest in them.
- <u>Remedy</u>: Turn judgment into curiosity, compliments, and compassion.

If you have a fear of coming off as nosy or intrusive, my guess is – no offense – on some level it's because your intention is nosy or intrusive.
In addition to feeling awful, judgment of others will keep a conversation stuck on boring small talk because people can sense your harsh thoughts and won't feel safe opening up to you. Going deeper, judgment of others is actually a fear of being judged yourself; I'll explain that one in a minute.

When you can listen to someone from a place of curiosity and compassion, you create that safe space for them to be vulnerable. This is very hard to fake; people can usually feel intentions on a sensory level.

So how do you come from a place of good intentions – especially if you're in a bad habit of judging (like I used to be)? Release those judgmental thoughts as they come up and flip them to positive.

Reframe: Releasing judgment about someone
allows me to show a genuine interest in them.

Note: You *Will* Judge

"Know that you cannot help but judge. What you then do with your judgment is the choice."
— Story Waters, author and spiritual teacher

I'll admit, I constantly make judgments about people – including myself. My Myers-Briggs personality type is INFJ, and you better believe that "J" stands for "Judging."

Judgments can be helpful – like applying your insight from a past experience to a present situation and using it to make a better decision.

When I say "release judgment" in your conversations, I mean don't hold your opinions and preferences *against* the other person. That means whatever someone shares with you, be grateful for that gift. Don't use that new information to categorize them as inferior to you in any way; e.g. less deserving, less interesting, etc.

Releasing judgment does NOT mean you shouldn't have an opinion. You can acknowledge the difference between another person's situation and what you may have done differently; just don't hold that difference against them.

For example, maybe you think cauliflower is the nastiest vegetable to ever grow on the face of the earth. Does that mean you're "judging" it or someone who buys it?

Um, no. You're perfectly capable of passing by one of those little white bunches in the produce section, acknowledging it's not your favorite veggie, and being happy for the woman who just put one in her grocery cart. Zero judgment; just acknowledging a difference in produce preference.

Two Ways Fear of Judgment Manifests

Fear of judgment tends to manifest itself in two ways:

#1 When you *decide* what others are thinking
#2 When you're *dependent on* what others are thinking

#1 When you *decide* what others are thinking

It's human nature to assume everyone else views the world through the same lens you do. But one look at all the different political viewpoints, charities of choice, and endless variety of sushi rolls that exist, and it's clear we all have our own preferences. These endless options mean it's *impossible* to make a completely accurate decision about how or why someone else feels or thinks the way they do – especially how or why they think the way they do about *you*.

For instance, writing this book was an intense process that took months of isolation and creative focus in order to put twenty years of life lessons into a structure that was clear, helpful, and hopefully entertaining. One of the few times I went out during this heads-down period was to a family friend's party with my parents. My mom and dad could see firsthand how intense the writing process was and how much I was working on it, but they assumed that other people wouldn't "get it." So when I said I could only stay for a few hours before returning to writing, they encouraged me to create what they thought was a "socially acceptable" deadline for my manuscript – such as, "Let's tell people your manuscript is due this week so they'll understand why you had to leave the party early."

But that deadline wasn't true – which means not only did it go against my core value of honesty (even though it was 100% well-intentioned), it was *deciding for other people* what deadline would be "socially acceptable" to justify me leaving a party early. So if it was due in three days that was ample justification – but not if it was due in three weeks? Who cares! I was working on a huge project with an impending deadline and that's all that anyone else needed to know. They could think whatever they wanted about it, but I wasn't going to decide for them, nor care if they were upset if I left a party early to go work on it.

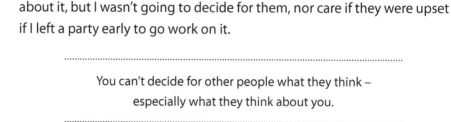

> You can't decide for other people what they think –
> especially what they think about you.

Your job is not to decide what other people must be thinking or to adjust your words and actions in accordance with that (false) assumption. *Chapter II: Effortless Engagement* was dedicated to doing the exact opposite: being your consistent self with everyone and letting *them* figure out how they want to react to you. Besides, do you really want to be responsible for other people's thoughts and decisions, even if you could control them (which you can't anyway)? No way.

Going even further, most of what people tend to think about you is secretly what they think about *themselves* – and good luck trying to control someone's thoughts about themselves!

Years ago, a man I'd never met stumbled across my website and sent me an email that harshly judged himself (by saying he was undesirable) and me (by saying the only reason I had luck meeting men was because I was pretty). He stated I was incapable of teaching other women how to meet men because I couldn't relate to them.

Clearly, he hadn't read any of my three-hundred testimonials and success stories that showed all the results I'd helped women achieve. But I knew his email wasn't about me at all, it was about his own rough judgments of himself. So I told him that. Here's part of my response to him:

"Please don't make judgments about people (including yourself) on behalf of others. That's not your responsibility – and I guarantee it will only continue to lead you to unhappy, self-fulfilling prophecies. Let people make decisions about you and others in their own time and way. And then you can decide whether you agree with them or not, and whether or not you care about their opinion. But please don't skip ahead and make that decision for them."

Your only responsibilities in creating a connection are to show up as your authentic self and to be curious about the other person. That's it. Being your authentic self puts out a unique signal for the right people to find you and for the wrong people to be naturally repelled. It's a beautiful process.

#2 When you're *dependent on* what others are thinking

"Be who you are and say what you feel, because those who mind don't matter and those who matter don't mind."
    – Dr. Seuss, children's author

If you're constantly afraid of what other people think about you, you've probably found the advice to "stop caring about other people" to be extremely unhelpful. As a human, you can't just stop caring – and honestly, you shouldn't. The world would be an awful place if no one cared about anyone. What you can and should stop caring about is *what people think about you.*

....

You should care about other people –
just not what they think about you.

....

This is a tiny but mighty shift in thought. As mentioned, people's reactions have little – if anything – to do with you anyway, and the people you choose to surround yourself with better not be ones who judge you. Who wants someone like that in their life?

The (Surprising) Root of All Judgment

"If you hate a person, you hate something in him that is part of yourself. What isn't part of ourselves doesn't disturb us."
    – Hermann Hesse, German novelist

So where's all this judgy-ness coming from?

It's impossible to be a harsh critic of others while fully and unconditionally loving yourself. That means the root of your judgment is always insecurity about yourself. Likely, some sort of internal wound, void, or trauma within you hasn't fully healed, so it continues to rear its ugly head in the form of self-judgment.

When you need a break from judging yourself, or when an opportunity pops-up (Hello, Facebook!), you'll turn that judgment on others. This gives you a temporary reprieve from beating yourself up, but until you address your own deeper insecurities, you'll always turn that judgment back on yourself.

This brutal cycle of "judge myself, judge others, judge myself" directly translates to your fear of being judged by other people. Again, it's human nature to assume that whatever you think, everyone else is thinking too.

....

> When you judge others, you assume your harsh thoughts
> about them are the same ones they're thinking about you.

....

It's a never-ending loop that feels awful, repels good people, and isn't even based on reality!

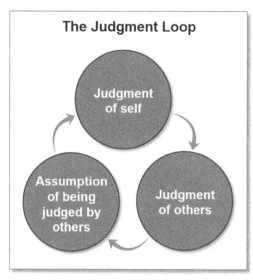

Three Steps to Stop Judging

So how do you break the Judgment Loop? Just follow these three steps...

1) Catch it and go deeper
2) Channel into curiosity, a compliment, or compassion
3) Rinse and repeat

First, understand where your own insecurity is coming from so you can start healing that wound. Next, channel any lingering judgments into curiosity, a compliment, or compassion. Finally, rinse and repeat until that way of thinking becomes a natural reflex every time a negative thought about someone else – or yourself – enters your mind.

Channeling your negative thoughts into positive ones will feel so much better because judging *always* feels crappy. Also, when you start to think nice thoughts about other people, you subconsciously start to assume that they're thinking nice thoughts about you too.

A scientific process called "neuroplasticity" enables your brain to adopt a new thought habit like this. You can create a new neural pathway (i.e. way of thinking) by catching your undesired thoughts as they pop-up and redirecting them into thoughts that support what you desire to be thinking instead. The pathways get stronger with repetition and eventually, they can become your new normal.

1) Catch it + go deeper

To reveal the root of the insecurity that's causing your judgment, start noticing those negative thoughts the moment they happen. For example, maybe you see a woman boldly sporting a bright yellow dress and catch yourself thinking:

- *"Who wears something like that? What a weirdo."*
- *"She must want a lot of attention. She's trying way too hard."*
- *"I wouldn't be caught dead in a dress like that."*

Going deeper, thoughts like those might come from a place of jealousy about this woman who has the confidence to wear something eye-catching and is comfortable standing out from the crowd. That could trigger your fear at the thought of being judged by others if you wore the same dress because you assume they'd have the same critical thoughts about you that you're having about her right now. So instead of acknowledging your fears or jealousy, it's easier to turn them into a not-so-nice thought about the woman.

Note: jealousy can be a powerful way to reveal desires that you may not have been consciously aware of until you see someone or something that triggers them to become a conscious thought – so listen to it.

Whatever the reason for your critical thoughts about this woman, accept that they aren't truly about her and move on to the next step.

2) Channel into curiosity, a compliment, or compassion

"Compliments are you emitting real energy – and when it's genuine, the other person vibrates at a rate that makes them shine."
    – Robert Kerr, Scottish author

Once you catch a judgmental thought, channel it into curiosity, a compliment, or compassion. When you start actively seeking out the good in people – and there is *always* something good – you create a new habit of looking for the positive which overrides your habit of jumping to judgment.

> Channel judgments about others into curiosity, a compliment, or compassion and self-judgment will melt away.

Find something you like about the other person or assume a good thought about them. In the example of the woman in the yellow dress, here's what channeling those statements might look like:

- Curiosity: *"I wonder where she got that cool dress."*
- Compliment: *"What a beautiful dress, maybe I should add yellow to my wardrobe."*
- Compassion: *"Good for her, the world needs more women who aren't afraid to make a bold clothing statement!"*

Major bonus points if you go share your positive thought with her -- and truly mean it as you say it:

- Curiosity: *"I love your dress. Where'd you get it?"*
- Compliment: *"Just want to say your dress is beautiful."*
- Compassion: *"Bravo for wearing a bold color. The world needs more sunshine yellow!"*

Making someone feel good will automatically make you feel good and can start building a new positive thought habit ("neural pathway") turning negative thinking patterns into positive ones.

> The more positive thoughts you have about others, the more positive thoughts you'll assume they have about you.

The more you practice, the faster you'll begin to see the world through a new lens of kindness, as opposed to one of constant criticism. Believe me when I say that this new way of positive thinking will feel incredible and change your life in ways you can't even imagine.

Plus, when you extend compassion to someone first, they're much more likely to extend it back to you. So give others what you yourself want to receive from them, and then you can both enjoy the gift exchange.

3) Rinse and repeat

As channeling judgment into positive thoughts becomes your new way of being, every person you talk to will feel that and open up to you even more, which will make your conversations a lot more interesting and personal. You, like everyone, can feel when you're being judged by someone. And even though you may logically *know* that judgment has nothing to do with you (i.e. everything to do with the person judging) it still *feels* crappy and can prevent a real connection.

On top of that, releasing your judgment helps liberate you from constantly worrying about what other people think about you, freeing you up to move through the world without the weight of that insecurity. This creates a new Judgment Loop that can become your new, even more fabulous way of being.

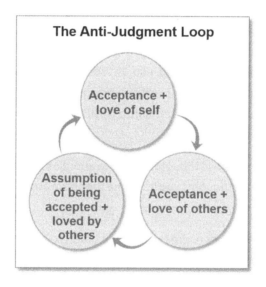

When you put on a performance – i.e. start acting outside of your authentic self, usually for purposes of achieving a certain outcome – that's when the deep fear sets in that someone will "see through your façade" and call you out on being fake.

When you are simply your natural self around everyone and in every situation, there's no performance to judge and no façade to risk crumbling. You simply bring an uninhibited energy to every interaction – the same energy you would use in deciding which bunch of bananas to buy at the grocery store (yep, another produce analogy!).

Imagine yourself in the produce section of the store, picking out bananas. Would it even cross your mind that someone might judge you based on your selection?

> *"Look at the weird bunch of bananas that woman just put in her cart – what a loser!"*

Of course not. You're picking out freakin' bananas – there's literally *nothing to judge*. You're not turning anything "on," which means you're not putting on a performance that's subject for review by others.

You're just doing your thing. If someone doesn't like it, who cares? When being your consistent self becomes your default way of being, you don't have to think twice about what to say, what do, or what other people think about any of it. It is simply what it is.

Action Items

1. Describe a recent situation where you felt yourself judging another person.
2. How did it feel to have those thoughts about them?
3. Going deeper, how might those thoughts have actually been about yourself?
4. How can you channel those thoughts into a compliment, curiosity, or compassion about the other person?
5. How can you reframe that thought into a compliment, curiosity, or compassion about yourself?

Why Your Words Are a Mirror

Here's a little secret: the words you use to describe other people get *applied to you* by the people listening to you.

For instance, if you say to your coworker Nathan:

"My friend Amara is so thoughtful; she always knows what to say to make me feel better."

Nathan will subconsciously associate "thoughtful" and "makes me feel better" with *you*. So basically, the more you talk-up others, the better you look. But it's got to be authentic.

Keep in mind, this process works the same way for negative traits. When you use critical words to describe another person, anyone within earshot will subconsciously associate the negative qualities with you. Plus, if you speak negatively about people behind their back, the person you're talking to is going to wonder what you say about *them* behind their back too. So, releasing judgment not only creates a stronger connection, but it can make you look good to other people too.

Be Open Past the First Impression

A client of mine, Wendy, used to work as a Teacher's Assistant at a university. In one of her classes, she admitted that her first impression of the students – most of whom were in their 50's and 60's – was that they didn't look very interesting or engaged. But once Wendy started grading their research papers, she quickly changed her mind and said…

"I found out they were so smart and interesting! How they're thinking, their insight, what they're capable of, it was amazing! And I couldn't tell that by simply looking at them. Lesson learned: let people surprise you."

You'll always have an initial assessment about someone when you first meet them, which is usually based on information from your past experiences with others who they remind you of. The key is to be open to letting that first impression change as you gather more information about the person, because it's likely that at least some – if not all – of what you think about them is incorrect.

Even after connecting with thousands of people over the years, I still love to let people surprise me and change my initial impression of them. Releasing judgment will also open the door to discover a whole new world of truly phenomenal men I guarantee you've been missing. Once you take the time to get to know them beyond their appearance and choice of icebreaker, you might find a total gem that you would have otherwise missed at first glance.

Element 5: Share Insights and Stories

"We cultivate love when we allow our most vulnerable and most powerful selves to be deeply seen and known."
— Dr. Brené Brown, professor and author

- <u>Fear</u>: *"I don't want to come off braggy."*
- <u>Symptom</u>: Conversation feels like an interview.
- <u>Reframe</u>: Equally contributing insights and stories deepens the connection and reveals compatibility.
- <u>Remedy</u>: Contribute to the conversation as topics naturally come up and with zero expectation/need for validation.

If you have a major fear of being seen as braggy, my guess is that you're completely repelled by people who brag.

When we see someone acting in a way that totally turns us off, our natural reaction is to do the complete opposite of that behavior, so we don't inflict those feelings of annoyance or repulsion on others.

The problem with this approach is when people take that avoidance to the opposite extreme. For example, if you loathe bragging, in an effort to create as much distance between you and that behavior, you might not talk about yourself *at all*.

But going to any extreme always has its own downsides, which include, but are not limited to:

- Conversations turn into interviews (e.g. rapid-firing questions).
- Conversations get stuck at surface-level (people won't open up to someone who isn't also opening up).
- People feel as though you're hiding something.
- People think you're boring (because you're not sharing anything).
- You leave no lasting impression on anyone.
- People will use you as a sounding board to simply talk *at* you.
- People will place little value on you, your time, and your energy because you haven't given them any reason to do so.

....

Reframe: Contributing my own insights and stories
deepens the connection and reveals compatibility.

....

Instead of never talking about yourself and always making the conversation about the other person, move closer to the middle of the Sharing Spectrum and become an active participant in the conversation.

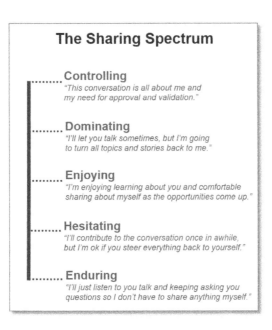

The Sharing Spectrum

Controlling
"This conversation is all about me and my need for approval and validation."

Dominating
"I'll let you talk sometimes, but I'm going to turn all topics and stories back to me."

Enjoying
"I'm enjoying learning about you and comfortable sharing about myself as the opportunities come up."

Hesitating
"I'll contribute to the conversation once in awhile, but I'm ok if you steer everything back to yourself."

Enduring
"I'll just listen to you talk and keeping asking you questions so I don't have to share anything myself."

Find this balance by simply showcasing your own relevant insights and stories as they *naturally* come up in conversation and releasing your need for validation from the other person. I'll show you how, coming up.

Action Items

1. Based on how much you tend to contribute to conversations, where would you place yourself on the Sharing Spectrum?
2. Why do you feel like you share that much (or that little)?

The Crucial Benefits of Contributing to the Conversation

"When two givers indulge in a connection, it's like magic. It's alchemy. I water you; you water me. We never drain each other, we just grow."
     – Unknown

If you're like many of the women I help, there's a good chance you're closer to the Hesitating or Enduring end of the Sharing Spectrum. But contributing your own insights and stories is the crucial final element required to create a meaningful connection.

Connection goes both ways: you must experience
another person *and* let them experience you.

Before I show you how to move toward the middle of the Sharing Spectrum, here's a list of the incredible benefits you'll get by speaking up a little more…

★ You'll naturally screen out the wrong people/men

When you show others even small glimpses of who you are, you'll quickly learn who "your people" are based on how their reaction makes you feel. For example, if you just revealed your love of Disney princess movies to a woman and were met with a, "What a weirdo" look from her, note it. In reading this book you're doing the work to release judgment and think positive thoughts about others, so the last thing you want in your circle of influence is someone who's doing the opposite.

"Fail Fast" is a mantra used in the entrepreneur world. It means to find the business approaches and systems that *don't work*, so you can move on to discover the ones that do work and focus on those instead. Applying this to conversations, filter out people who don't make you feel good as quickly as possible – especially the wrong men, *before* you get emotionally attached to them.

It's a gift to quickly discover that a man you're talking to doesn't have the potential to be the right guy, so you can turn your attention to the ones who do. If he's not right for you, he's probably perfect for someone else, so set him free to go find her (or him!).

★ You'll reveal potential compatibility

"Your vocalization of passion and compassion helps others do the same."
– Shawn Achor, happiness expert and author

In addition to screening out the wrong people, purposefully exhibiting and discussing the traits you desire in a partner naturally attracts people with those same traits and values to you like a magnet. It's like putting out your own custom "Bat Signal" and calling in specific people meant to be in your life.

Showcase the traits that you want to attract in others
so the right people can find you.

Speaking of bats, did you know there are over 900 species of bats in the world? When I learned that fun fact at a zoo exhibit, I asked the zookeeper, "How does each type of bat find each other?" She said each species has their own unique call, and I realized that was the same concept as showcasing your unique personality so the right people could find you!

Sometimes in order to get off the surface level topics, you have to be the first one to share something meaningful and/or a little vulnerable. Most people don't know how to naturally segue into a deeper level of conversation, so when you share about yourself it subconsciously invites the other person to do the same. This not only makes for great conversation, but naturally reveals potential compatibility between you two – whether for purposes of romance, friendship, work, or anything in between.

★ You'll bond faster with the right people/men

Contributing your own personal topics to a conversation helps potential partners bond with you over shared interests and/or curiosity about them. It also shows men that you have room in your life for them. This subconsciously plants the seed for them to start picturing themselves with you – and it can be done in your very first conversation.

For instance, you're at the bus stop talking with the man standing next to you. The topic of travel comes up and you say, "I love traveling to different countries but hate the planning part – like researching airfares and booking hotels. I just want to show up in an exotic place and immediately have everything ready for me to start exploring."

Well, maybe that man *loves* the planning part of travel and responds with, "Well if we ever traveled together, I'm happy to be the planner – I love scouring all the travel hacking websites."

Or, maybe he also dislikes the planning aspects, so you both agree that if you ever travel together, you're hiring a travel agent to take care of those details. Sharing about yourself and your preferences, even something small like not enjoying the logistics of travel, is a fun way to learn about someone, let them learn about you, and create a fun bonding moment thinking about your hypothetical trip together. Which may one day become a real trip together, you never know!

★ You'll get comfortable with being vulnerable

If you want your future partner to love and accept you for who you are, you must *show* him who you are from the very first conversation. You can start by sharing new aspects about yourself with people currently in your life.

By practicing your vulnerability and connection skills now, not only will it give your conversations more depth and speed-up the process of finding the right man, it'll give you a chance to get comfortable with revealing those aspects to your future man. By the time you find yourself in a relationship, you will have already found your groove with contributing to conversations, so expressing your needs and expectations to your partner will feel easier.

★ You'll keep the conversation naturally flowing

Being able to confidently and comfortably talk about yourself to others also ensures you'll always have something interesting to contribute to a conversation. If you're forced to rely on other people to do all the talking, it gives all the power to (and puts pressure on) them. That will either make them uncomfortable – because they're now forced to carry the entire conversation – or they'll start using you as a sounding board. Either way, this means you're now at the mercy of whatever they want to talk about for however long they want to talk about it.

★ You'll be continually reminded of how awesome you are

It can be easy to forget your own value and self-worth if you don't make it a point to continually remind yourself. A great way to do that? Contributing your own stories, insights, and opinions to conversations. This serves as a powerful reminder to *yourself* that you're an awesome person who's living a fun, interesting, and amazing life.

How to Comfortably Contribute

Once you get comfortable contributing insights and stories as they naturally pop-up, you'll make a truly memorable impression on people. People can feel when you're not seeking their validation and simply sharing a story for purposes of contributing to the conversation.

Here are nine approaches to practice sharing about yourself with others in any conversation:

#1 Create a repertoire of your favorite topics and stories

Make note of a few topics, interests, hobbies, or causes that you're naturally drawn to and start building a repertoire of your favorites that you can call upon any time.

My personal go-to topics are entrepreneurship, international travel, and relationships. If I can naturally steer a conversation to any of these topics, not only will I have a lot of stories and insights to contribute, I know I'll likely learn something new about them from the other person's thoughts and experiences they share.

Action Items

1. List three topics that you love talking about.
2. List three stories from your life that you're proud of and/or love talking about.
3. Write down a few details of those stories to help them come alive as you share in the conversation.

#2 Gather daily insights and personal anecdotes

A great way to always have something new and interesting to share comes from simply being present as you go about your daily life. Notice the colors, the textures, the people, and the random insights that pop in your head. It could be a big event or a tiny detail that you noticed. Refer to the Seven Ways to Snap into the Present from *Chapter I: Magnetic Approachability* for more ways to be present in the moment.

For example, you're at a deli and see a green Jell-O salad. Maybe your first thought is "Poor Slimer from *Ghostbusters* went through a blender." Crack yourself up with your awesome sense of humor! Maybe later you'll find yourself in a conversation with a man who asks "How's your day going?" and you can share the anecdote, "I went to this cute little deli downtown and the Jell-O salad looked like Slimer met his demise in a KitchenAid." Showing your weird side always makes conversations more fun and interesting, as well as attracts the right people to you who adore and accept you.

Maybe you're into fashion and saw a woman sporting a red cape at the coffee shop this morning and made a mental note of it. Later that day you're talking to a female coworker when the topic of fashion comes up and you share your insight, "I saw a woman with a red cape today and thought, 'I need a cape in my life.'" Et voila! Now you're talking about fashion and capes.

> Contributing anecdotes and insights adds depth to your life and inspires you to notice the extraordinary details.

#3 Create a purposeful juxtaposition

What's one of the quickest ways to become intriguing? Share two very different aspects of yourself that seem almost contradictory with each other and watch people try to figure you out. Getting information that seemingly conflicts with each other will make them wonder what other interesting facts you harbor.

> Sharing two different sides of yourself that don't immediately "match up" creates instant intrigue.

Here's an example. One of my clients, Amanda, was dressing for confidence and conversation by wearing a pretty blue skirt to the grocery store. As she pulled into a parking spot, a cute guy pulled into the spot next to her. He had a bike rack on his car, so he was clearly outdoorsy, which she is too. But suddenly, she lost her confidence and felt inauthentic because the way she was dressed didn't reflect that sporty side of her.

I told her that was a *great* thing! She had the opportunity to create an authentic juxtaposition between the way she was dressed (which showed she cared about her appearance) and her athletic interests (which showed she had a love of biking). Think about it. If you're dolled up looking and feeling great and let slip "I have a [insert cool bike brand] and love to go riding on the weekend," in one sentence you've just become an outdoorsman's DREAM WOMAN. You can dress up like a lady *and* race down a mountainside on a bike? Yes-please-can-I-take-you-out-tonight?

What you're wearing doesn't change who you are as a person, so don't hide or "play down" one side of yourself simply because your outer appearance doesn't happen to reflect that in the moment. Instead, purposefully play-up the juxtaposition so you can create an instant fascination. One of my clients Rose loves this approach. She'll share her beliefs when the topic of religion naturally arises, then purposefully steer on the subject of music she so can also showcase her love of hip-hop.

Besides, if someone "can't handle" that their initial assessment of you conflicts with the new information you just introduced to the conversation, they aren't your person anyway. You want people in your life who are open-minded and interested in getting to know you beyond your outer appearance. What better way to do that than to show one side of yourself on the outside, and then purposefully bring up another authentic side of yourself in the conversation?

It's fun to keep people curious and guessing – especially men you're interested in. Men love the thrill that comes with not being able to figure a woman out, so go ahead and give it to them. Let them know there's more to you than meets the eye – and they need to get your phone number to find it out.

Sharing seemingly-conflicting information can also serve as a powerful reminder for people to not judge a book by its cover. If they had you pegged as a certain type of person based solely on how you were dressed, your gender, your ethnicity, or any other external aspect, then surprise them with seemingly contradictory information. This plants the thought that perhaps they shouldn't jump to conclusions so quickly about the next person.

#4 Humanize yourself

"Being vulnerable allows you to become memorable. We feel strongly connected to those who allow us to be vulnerable around them."
    – AJ Harbinger, co-host of "The Art of Charm" podcast

Some people try too hard to make a great first impression in an attempt to receive the validation they can't give themselves. My client Elizabeth calls them "Try-Hards." To differentiate yourself from those who are constantly seeking permission and acceptance from others, showcase your softer side. It will feel good revealing that you're ok being seen as an imperfect human (just like everyone else is) and helps others drop their guard too, giving way for a real connection to bloom.

....

It feels good to show people you're an imperfect human
and gives them permission to do the same.

....

Here are some ways to show your human side:

- Share a life lesson you recently learned.
- Share something you regret doing or saying (and what you would do differently next time).
- Share a time when your judgment of someone was wrong.
- Share an aspect of your life that you're currently improving.
- Share a goal you've set and the steps you're taking to achieve it.
- Share something you don't know how to do but wish you did.
  - Bonus: This plants the seed that you have room in your life for someone else *and* that you're into self-development.
- Ask for the other person's advice about something (including any of the above).

Sharing anything along these lines sets a different tone for the conversation and shows the other person you're not trying to impress them or get their validation. It shows that you're comfortable and confident with yourself, and you don't take yourself too seriously.

Constantly having to show-off or brag about your accomplishments reveals deep insecurity. It takes *more* confidence to show the vulnerable sides of yourself and truly feel okay, regardless of how those aspects are received by another person.

An example of a "humanizing" but not-too-vulnerable story could be that time you attempted a recipe for dulce de leche bars when, in gathering all the ingredients at the store, you somehow forgot to buy the dulce de leche (oops, my bad).

Or the time you were out with a friend and her coworkers, and one of them sent a drink over to you – but you blew him off because you were shy and didn't know what to say, and had always felt bad about that. Then years later when you were scrolling through your phone and came across his name, you sent him an apology text – which is exactly what I did:

People want to connect with someone who is just as human as they are; someone they can relate to and grow with. Having a partner who's "perfect" only serves to put pressure on *themselves* to be perfect. So show your human side whenever possible, which gives the other person permission to show theirs so you two can create a bond even faster.

But don't go too far on the "humanizing" spectrum into self-deprecation territory. It's unattractive and screams, "Please validate me!" which is a conversation no one is going to want to continue unless they're a controlling, emotional abuser.

#5 Aim for concepts, not people

"Great minds discuss ideas; average minds discuss events; small minds discuss people."
 – Eleanor Roosevelt, social activist and former First Lady

I recommend kicking-off your conversation contribution by sharing a story about an event or activity and then moving into the deeper concept or emotion behind it. The goal here is to avoid getting on the topic of another person or group of people because that's a slippery slope to Gossipville – i.e. a fast way to create an anti-meaningful conversation laden with judgment.

#6 Show, don't tell

Go for depth over breadth by choosing a single aspect within a topic and then going deeper on it. Put another way: instead of answering a question or contributing to a topic with a laundry list of examples, choose one example and share the details and emotions you were experiencing in it.

For instance, if someone asks if you like to travel, naming off the past twenty countries you've been to will make it hard to steer into a meaningful conversation because the amount of different ways that conversation can now go feels completely overwhelming. Plus, going for quantity over quality comes off as bragging, which can turn the conversation into an unenjoyable competition.

Instead, respond with a story about one of your favorite destinations and invite the other person into that experience, as you discovered how to do with the Empathic Listening Technique in Element 3. Paint the picture. Give them context. Get descriptive; the story is in the details! For example:

> *"I've traveled a lot, but my favorite trip was a safari in Kenya. Growing up, I loved animals and we'd always go to the zoo; but seeing them in the wild was so much better. One of my favorite moments was when a huge lion sauntered up to our car window…"*

This approach invites the other person into your story with relatable topics (childhood, zoo, travel) but still interesting stories and new information (Kenya, safari, lion).

Go even deeper by sharing *why* you loved it, what you learned, and how it changed your life. Much more interesting!

#7 Take someone back to the moment

Describe a specific moment in time by adding context and a few vivid details. It will help bring people back to the moment with you and add instant depth to the conversation. The goal is to bring them into your life by giving them a visual description of the person, place, and/or thing that isn't there in the moment with you two.

The more interesting and relevant details you provide, the more directions you naturally give the conversation to go without being overwhelming. Each detail becomes a potential jumping-off point for the other person to have their own insight, opinion, or be reminded of a similar story in their own life. People tend to be comfortable with parameters; it reduces the feeling of overwhelm, which is a gift in our age of information overload.

Also, keep some pictures on your phone that relate to your favorite topics and stories of choice so you can bring people into the story even more – like the lady serving hummus samples did for me.

#8 Ask questions that you want to be asked back to you

As you discovered in the first element of a meaningful conversation, asking questions and introducing topics that *you* want to talk about helps you stay engaged in the conversation. It's also a great way to authentically showcase your awesome self!

When you ask someone a question, chances are they're going to ask that same question back to you, which allows you to share your relevant stories and thoughts.

For instance, if you love movies a good way to introduce that topic is to ask a question about it, like:

- *"Have you seen any interesting movies lately?"*
- *"Any new movies you're looking forward to?"*
- *"I'm looking for movies to add to my watch list, what's one of your favorites?"*
- *"What's the weirdest movie you've ever seen?"*

It's a topic that you enjoy, but you're not sharing your own experiences or preferences with it yet. You're letting the other person go first, knowing that question will more than likely come back to you eventually and give you free rein to share-away.

#9 Talk about the future

If you can't come up with something interesting offhand, introduce your plans or thoughts about the future. Talk about what you're looking forward to, such as your weeklong Hawaiian vacation once your big work project is finally done, or your nephew's birthday party on Saturday. Share your daydreams, what you're most excited about – the thoughts, questions, even fears that run through your head while you're lying in bed trying to fall asleep. Those topics alone will give you plenty of things to talk about, will keep the conversation interesting, and can help you process those thoughts out loud.

Talking about the future will also put you in a good mood by reminding yourself about all the interesting and exciting things yet to come! Maybe one afternoon you were flipping through *Vogue*, came across a gorgeous blue pea coat and told yourself someday you're going to own one. Bring that up in conversation; it shows that you put thought into what you want in life, whether it's a big goal or small desire. The simple fact that you're thinking about what you want is incredibly sexy. Even sexier is sharing the steps you're taking to get it.

So instead of just saying, "I want to go to Europe someday," which is an instantly forgettable statement, describe which European country is at the top of your list, what you want to do there, and why you chose it. Such as:

> *"I want to take a train into Ljubljana to visit the castle on the hill and watch the Slovenian pipers!"*

Now THAT'S a memorable statement that makes you instantly interesting *and* will get you excited about it in the moment. You can also bet the next time Slovenia pops up in a conversation, the person you said that sentence to will instantly think of you. Just make sure you have a genuine intention to do the things you talk about. Don't fall into the trap of "all talk, no walk" like we covered earlier in the chapter; it's a major turn-off.

Declining a Question

"Just because someone asks you a question doesn't mean you have to answer it."

– Bethenny Frankel, *I Suck at Relationships So You Don't Have To*

You have every right to decline answering a question, even if it was asked with the best of intentions. Here are some ways to politely move the conversation away from a topic or question you don't want to talk about:

- *"It's a long story I'd rather not get into."*
- *"Thanks for asking, but it's not something I enjoy talking about."*
- *"That's not my favorite subject...tell me more about your trapeze business."*

Say each response with a smile, then immediately ask a question back to the other person so they know they didn't offend you to the point of wanting to end the conversation. Unless they did offend you to that point; in which case, jump back to "How to Keep it Going – Or Shut it Down" in *Chapter II: Effortless Engagement* for simple scripts on how to exit the conversation.

Contributing vs Bragging

"I got no secret purpose
I don't seem obvious...
...do I?"
    – Jimmy Eat World, "The Authority Song"

Intention is the foundation of every connection. If your intention behind sharing something is to get a certain reaction out of the person you're talking to, just don't say it. It won't feel good and they will likely sense your "secret purpose" for saying it.

Years ago, I felt like I needed to prove to people that I was interesting. Which, of course, stemmed from feeling like I *wasn't* interesting, so I constantly searched for external validation to prove it wrong. If I had instead worked on validating myself and accepting that I've lived a good life and have some great stories to share, I wouldn't have needed that approval from others.

This insecurity showed up in my conversations when I'd insert a topic I knew I could brag about, or share a fact that made me look smart – even if it was completely unrelated to the topic at hand. Every time I did it, it felt awful and pathetic.

Plus, in a sad twist of irony, the people who I wanted to impress – the ones who were genuinely interesting and secure enough to not brag about it – would be completely turned off when I did this. People can almost always feel when you're bragging.

I eventually became so turned-off with my approach that there was a period where I completely stopped talking about myself at all, and just asked other people questions. But I soon realized the drawbacks of this other extreme end of the Sharing Spectrum. I've since found a good balance of contributing to conversations as topics naturally come, with only genuine intentions, as well as giving myself the validation I want instead of seeking it from other people.

If you catch yourself needing approval from others, ask yourself these questions:

- *What reaction am I hoping to get from the other person?*
- *If I do get that reaction, how will I feel?*
- *If I don't get that reaction, how will I feel?*
- *Why do I need that reaction?*
- *How can I give that appreciation and validation to myself instead?*

Now that you know the Five Elements of a Meaningful Conversation, you have the power to turn any conversation into the chance for a fulfilling connection, no matter who it's with, how long it is, or what the topic is. As a recap, here are the Five Elements again:

1) Ask Awesome Questions
2) Hold Space for Silence
3) Listen Like Your Life Depends Upon It
4) Release Judgment
5) Share Insights and Stories

How to Seal the Deal

Once you've created a meaningful connection with a man, getting him to ask you out is the easy part.

The best way is to naturally guide the conversation toward activities you two can do together on a date. I'll show you exactly how to do this coming up, including a few examples.

If that approach doesn't work (e.g. he doesn't get the hint or is still too shy to ask you out), I'll give you two more ways to ensure that, if he's truly interested, you two will walk away from your interaction with each other's phone numbers.

Here's Why It Needs to Be an Actual Date

When you're interested in a man, it's important to eventually go on an actual date together – which, ideally, he takes the lead in planning.

A date could honestly be any activity you two do together: dinner reservations at a restaurant, going to a movie, taking a walk on the beach. It's not about how much money is spent; it's about the thoughtfulness that goes into the experience. One of my best dates ever was when a man packed a blanket, sandwiches, and a bottle of wine and took me to a movie in the park under the stars. Simple, but well planned out and incredibly thoughtful.

Going out on an actual date not only makes you feel like a desired woman, but it also prevents a "situationship" from forming – a term which can defined as indefinitely hanging out with each other sans actual commitment or steps in the direction of commitment. If a man has no interest in being in a relationship, you want that to be revealed ASAP, so you don't waste another second on a man who's unable to give you what you truly want.

Also, as I learned the hard way, if you have to ask a man to take you out on a date, he's not the man for you. I've only had to do this once in my life, with a man I was "exploring a connection with" long-distance. Not only was it extremely uncomfortable to ask, but he got offended! That was the last straw in a string of red flags I had chosen to ignore up to that point. I love doing nice things for people and I knew I needed a man who enjoyed the same.

Remember, the meeting and dating phase is a man being on his best behavior, trying to impress you. That means if red flags are popping up now, trust that those are only the tip of the iceberg.

Three Ways to Get a Date with Him

Going in for "the ask" can be a scary experience for even the most confident of men. So if you want him to ask you out, you'll likely need to give him a glaring green light and make it as easy as possible. Here are the three ways to turn your meaningful conversation into an exchange of digits and a date:

#1 Inspire Him to Ask You Out

The fastest and most natural way to have a man ask you out is by steering the conversation toward activities, hobbies, places, and interests – i.e. potential dates you can go on together. When a topic comes up that you genuinely enjoy, or are curious about, jump on it! Show your excitement so he knows you're into it and he can channel that energy into the courage to ask you out.

Example 1
- Steer the conversation toward local favorites/hobbies/places
  - You: *"What do you do for fun?"*
  - Him: *"I'm excited to start playing more tennis this summer."*
- When something comes up you also like – jump on it!
  - You: *"No way, I play too – I just got my racket restrung!"*
- Sets up the opportunity to do something you both enjoy
  - Him: *"We should play together sometime – are you free Sunday?"*

Example 2

- Steer the conversation toward local favorites/hobbies/places
  - You: *"So, what's your favorite type of food in the city?"*
  - Him: *"I love barbeque, and just heard about a great new brisket place on the South Side."*
- When something comes up you also like – jump on it!
  - You: *"I love barbeque!"*
- Sets up the opportunity to do something you both enjoy
  - Him: *"Well, let's go check it out together!"*

This authentic approach makes it easy for him to pick a date place that he knows you'll enjoy. Plus, he'll think that asking you to go there was totally his idea, so he'll feel proud of himself. If you've taken the time to create a meaningful connection with a man, it truly can be *that* simple and easy to get him to ask you out (assuming he's interested and available).

Give him an extra second – literally

Just remember that most men are afraid of rejection, so give him a little bit of time to get to the ask-out. Sometimes he just needs an extra second to find the courage to say the words out loud.

For example, I was at an Aloe Blacc concert with a girlfriend a few years ago and spent most of the time talking to the cute guy standing next to me. At the end of the show, my friend and I were getting ready to leave, so I turned to him and said, "It was great meeting you. Unfortunately, I think my friend and I need to head out now." I purposefully made the sentence as long as possible to give him time to process what was happening and think of a way to get my phone number.

I could tell he was trying to come up with a way to ask because he had a, "Wait, don't go!" look in his eyes and his lips were pursed as if he was about to say something. So I just stood there and smiled for an extra second or two until he got the words together and said, "May I take you to dinner sometime?" I said yes, and we exchanged phone numbers.

On our date together, he asked me, "By the way, did you pause when you were leaving so I could ask you out?" I smiled and said, "Yep. You're welcome!" He loved *and* appreciated my little move.

Think of meeting and dating as a team sport. The man shouldn't bear the burden of doing everything; you have plenty of opportunities to help him along the way. Not only is a kind thing to do, but you'll both reap the benefits when you turn your conversation into a hot date with each other.

It may be subtle

Note: His ask-out might be very subtle, so listen carefully for it. Once again: most men are afraid of rejection, so asking you out indirectly can feel safer for them – but it's also easy for women to completely miss it.

This misfire happened twice in one night to a client of mine. We were out doing a wingwoman session, where we hit the town together so she could practice her social skills with me by her side. The first man we spoke to started telling us about a new Italian restaurant in the area that he'd read about. He casually said "Yeah, I've wanted to try it out. If only I had someone to go with." That last line was his safe and subtle ask-out to my client. If he'd been talking to me, I would have responded, "I love Italian, I'll go with you," and let him take it from there. But sadly, she totally missed it.

At the next venue, my client and I started talking to another man. A half-hour or so into the great conversation, he turned to her and said, "So, what are we doing this weekend?" Unfortunately, she took that as, "What are *you* doing this weekend," and proceeded to tell him about her plans to go shopping for a new furnace. Womp womp. Later I pointed out this was his playful way of asking her to do something with him this weekend.

Here are some examples of subtle ask-outs, so you can keep an eye out for them…

- *"If only I had someone to go with…"*
- *"What are we doing this weekend?"*
- *"That'd be fun to do sometime…"*

Watch for lines like those and then offer yourself up. You don't have to take the lead, simply say, "I'll do it with you!" or "Sounds fun, count me in." Done and done.

You've created a 100% safe space for him to ask for your number without risk of rejection and given him the go-ahead to plan the date – all in half a sentence.

Note: if you're interested in him and he asks you out for a certain date or time that doesn't work for you, be sure to suggest an alternative. If he's taken the lead and risked being rejected by you, it's time to meet him halfway and work together to set a date that you can both make.

#2 Put the Ball in His Court

You can lead a horse to water, but you can't make him drink. Or maybe the horse doesn't see the water. Or something else happens that prevents the horse from drinking it. Whatever. Anyway, if you steer the conversation toward mutual interests and he doesn't take advantage of the golden opportunity you've created to ask you out, help him by putting the ball in his court. Here's an example:

- Him: *"I love Peruvian food, there are some great places in the city."*
- You: *"Me too, I'm totally craving some ceviche."*
- Him: *"Mmmm, ceviche. I hear ya."*
- You: *"Well, if you ever want to grab some, I'm down."*

That way you've given him a clear signal (i.e. couldn't have made it any easier) that you'd like to get together, but it's still up to him to take the lead from there. Remember, there are amazing men out there who get nervous around incredible women like yourself and may need a little help asking you out. Maybe the man you're flirting with just had his heart broken. Or the last girl he dated used him for money, cheated on him, or worse. Be kind and help him out. That simple sentence might lead you into the arms of the love of your life.

The story of how I met a past boyfriend is a great example of this. The week before Halloween, I went to happy hour with some coworkers, and one invited his college roommate to join us. As soon as his friend showed up, I was completely smitten with Mr. Tall, Blonde, and Handsome.

We started chatting and I could tell he was shy – and single – but we hit it off. I had a feeling he might not have the courage to ask me out, so when the topic of Halloween came up, I told him about a charity costume party I was going to. He seemed interested, so I asked for his email address to forward the invitation to him. It was the perfect excuse to get my contact information into his hands without putting the pressure on him to ask me out in front of everyone, and without taking the lead to ask him out myself.

Sure enough, he emailed me back the next day. Somehow the Halloween event segued into the topic of turkey chili and our emails starting centering around who could make the best dish.

After a week of beating the turkey chili topic to death, he finally asked me out. On our first date he admitted that if I hadn't given him my email, he would have been too shy to reach out.

The important lesson here was that even though he didn't ask me out in the moment, I made sure he had a way to contact me so he could do it when he was ready. If you're interested in a man and adamant that he takes the lead in asking you on a date, use any excuse possible to get your contact information into his hands. Then have a little patience and give it a week or so.

You can also have a personal calling card to give people. My friend Ashlee used this approach with a card that showcased her love of t-shirt imprinting and baking fancy cakes, which also provided her contact information. She opted for a "half-size" business card style, so it had a personal aspect to it, instead of feeling like a formal business card...

Front

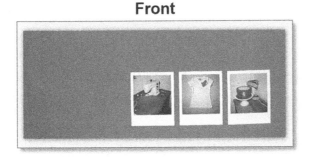

Back

If he asks for your business card, or you want to put the ball in his court by offering it to him, be sure to *hand-write* your cell phone number on the back. This small personal touch makes it clear you're not looking for a new business contact; you're interested in him personally.

#3 Ask Him Out

Full disclosure: asking a man out myself has never turned out well for me. But I know it's worked for other women, in some cases even leading to a few happy marriages, so it's always an option if the first two ask-out approaches don't work.

Just be prepared for how to handle what comes after that, which can be where things start to get confusing. Do you plan the date? Do you pay for it? What prevented him from asking you out despite you giving the cues you wanted him to? Is he truly interested in you or did he just agree to save face in the moment?

Note: I've been told by many men that they prefer to ask the woman out and plan the date. So if he hasn't asked you out after trying the first two approaches and you find yourself hoping he's interested, but deep down feeling like he may not be, listen to your gut and don't take the lead. It won't feel good. If you truly feel like he's interested in you and that he just isn't getting the hint or can't muster up the courage, then ask him out – and let me know how it goes.

Script: How I Got a Date on LinkedIn

Below is one of my most unusual ask-out stories. Since the entire conversation was captured online, it's a great word-for-word example of how I turned a case of mistaken identity into a date.

A few key notes on how I helped him ask me out:

- I never shut him down or made him feel creepy for reaching out (not even jokingly, it's too easy to get the tone wrong over technology).
- I always answered his questions with details, so he could build off them and share his own detailed experiences.
- I asked him questions.
- I purposefully introduced the "going out for food" topic, which made it easy for him to ask me out for lunch.

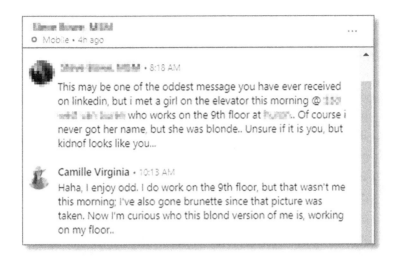

The Conversation (which played out over a week or so)…

- Simon: *This may be one of the oddest messages you have ever received on LinkedIn, but I met a girl on the elevator this morning @ west van buren who works on the 9th floor.. Of course I never got her name, but she was blonde.. Unsure if it is you, but kind of looks like you….*
- Me: *Haha, I enjoy odd. I do work on the 9th floor, but that wasn't me this morning. Now I'm curious who this blond version of me is, working on my floor.*
- Simon: *Awww, bummer that it isn't you…Well let's do some investigative work (Your twin was pretty)… Scan the floor for all blonde girls and we can do a lineup. I will also look out for you on the elevator now.*
- Me: *I'll keep an eye out. The nerve of her, stealing my looks!*
- Simon: *Yup, if I were you I would be super mad she's stealing your looks when you aren't here ;-)… So I see from your profile you have been all over the state/country, what brought you to Chicago?*
- Me: *I'm from Portland, Oregon originally and just moved here a few years ago and love it. Well, I had to adjust to a new definition of "cold" (we don't have negative degree anything in Oregon), but otherwise it's been great. Are you a transplant as well, or is the Midwest home for you?*
- Simon: *Yes, definitely a new definition of cold in the Midwest (frankly it sucks), but I do ski so at least we have that going for us.. Well I am a transplant, but I am only from northern WI so nowhere near as far away from home as you. I enjoy it here as well, definitely more to do*

here than home. How often are you able to go home? Do you live in the city or the burbs?

- Me: *I live in the city, I love being close to everything that is Chicago. I try to get back to Oregon twice a year; the summer is absolutely perfect out there. And so many outdoor things to do and see. Have you been skiing out west? Some big mountains there :)*
- Simon: *I actually went skiing on Saturday which was nice, in Wisconsin! How was your weekend?*
- Me: *Weekend was nice. On Friday we went to a new place in River North called Bavette's, great people watching and great old fashion craft cocktails. Very 1920's vibe.*
- Simon: *Sounds fun, I have never been to Bavette's, but I normally like those kinds of places where you can simply people watch and have a good time. So what do you normally do for lunch? I usually just head out by myself, if you ever wanted to go out around here count me in.*
- Me: *Sometimes I bring lunch, but I couldn't pull it together enough this weekend to manage that for this week. I'm up for lunch out sometime. :)*

More Tips for Your Conversational Arsenal

Now that you know the Five Elements of a Meaningful Conversation, here are a few more key tips to ensure you have everything you need to create a great connection with absolutely anyone.

Don't Say This to Him, or Anyone. Ever.

When in doubt, don't say something you wouldn't want to be said to you. Yes, that seems obvious, but it's baffling how many people don't follow the Golden Rule yet want others to do it for them (someone please explain that to me).

Specifically, below are four things *not* to say to someone who you want to create a connection with.

#1 Don't Be a Meanie

No matter how nervous you are or how long the awkward silence is, do not be mean to a man. Or anyone for that matter.

> No one likes to be around people who are mean,
> regardless of the reason. Because, duh.

Here's an example of what happens when you're mean, even "jokingly." I had a friend, Kara, who was very insecure. So much so that she couldn't even admit it, which meant it showed up in intense ways especially when it was challenged.

Whenever Kara and I were out and ended up talking to a man or group of men, she would always be abrasive and rude to them – which was her insecurities coming out. Her protective mode was to reject them before they could reject her. She would put them down, correct them, grill them, and become quite unpleasant whenever a man was around us. Which of course meant the men wouldn't be interested in her and usually leave shortly after engaging us.

Once they were gone, her reaction was always the same: "Men just can't handle me. I'm too intimidating for them!" Once I understood what was really going on, I finally responded, "Actually, it's because you're mean to them. I don't blame them for not wanting to be around that."

Unfortunately, that revelation didn't change her approach and eventually, she started being nasty to me too, which is when I ended the friendship. It's one of several examples I've experienced where someone's bad behavior to one person eventually gets applied to everyone else in their life.

Action Items

1. Describe a situation where you were mean or cold to someone for no particular reason.
2. What was the underlying fear or insecurity behind that?
3. How can you reframe that fear or insecurity and take a different approach next time?

#2 Start Light on the Intensity

If you have an edgy personality or dry sense of humor, start interactions off by showing your kindest side until the other person knows you aren't serious about the slightly harsh comments that come out of your mouth. Feel free to directly share that fun fact about yourself with them too.

- *"Forewarning: I have a weird sense of humor."*
- *"I can be a little sarcastic – but I'm a nice person, I promise."*
- *"I can't be held responsible for whatever comes out of my mouth when the Cubs are playing."*

The goal here is to leave zero room for misinterpretation. It's always a good idea to wait until the other person knows that your joke about [insert borderline offensive topic] is just for laughs and not your actual opinion or belief.

#3 Bridge the Gap (Don't Deepen the Divide)

"Likeness begets liking."

> – David Myers, *Social Psychology*

As you're talking, listen for aspects you have in common with the other person. Even the smallest detail, such as, "I love log-cabin-style tiny houses too!" The goal here is to avoid creating a divide between you and the other person, which can happen when you put them in a different category or assume they can't relate to you in some way.

For example, one night while out to dinner I overheard a man and a woman on what was clearly their first date – and it wasn't going well.

- Man: *"I just got back from two weeks in Japan, it was unreal. Have you been?"*
- Woman: *"Well, I actually used to live there, so my experience was totally different from yours."*

In one sentence, the woman instantly made the man and his experience inferior to hers – which I'm sure made him feel awesome and inspired him to keep talking about it. Just kidding. The man didn't know how to respond and ended up changing the subject. I'm also guessing that was the point he knew he didn't want to go out with her again.

Instead of immediately honing-in on the difference in their experiences, the woman could have used the common topic of Japan as a powerful bonding moment with him – like this:

- Man: *"I just got back from two weeks in Japan, it was unreal. Have you been?"*
- Woman: *"I love Japan, I used to live there. Tell me all about your trip!"*

Humans love to find things in common with each other, it satisfies our innate need for acceptance. So actively look for those commonalities, even if they're small, and then build off them with your conversation partner.

#4 No Self-Deprecation, Please. Thanks.

While I encourage you to humanize yourself, don't take that too far and become self-deprecating. Not only does it feel awful to say mean statements about yourself, but it reeks of massive insecurity.

People tend to be self-deprecating to control self-scrutiny by preemptively judging themselves before the other person can ("You can't judge me because I judged myself first! So there!"). Self-deprecation can come out in statements such as:

- *"You're going to think I'm a total freak, but…"*
- *"Can I be a pest and get change for a twenty?"*
- *"I don't want to hog the whole conversation by asking a question…"*

If this sounds a little too familiar to you, the quickest way to break the habit is to never say anything about yourself that you wouldn't say about another person.

....

Give yourself the same kindness
that you've been trying to give to everyone else.

....

Going a step further, that insecurity also needs to be healed on a deeper level. Try to discover the root of it, appreciate whatever it taught you and then release it. Figure out how you can start giving *yourself* the validation you've been craving from other people and quit hating on yourself. You're awesome, end of story. You just need to discover it – and creating conversations with others is a great way to do it.

How to Know When to Exit the Conversation

"Miss Ruth was a lady, and a lady always knows when to leave."
– Sipsey, *Fried Green Tomatoes*

As you get comfortable with creating meaningful connections, you'll be able to feel when a conversation is naturally coming to a close. Conversations – like everything – are energy, and when that energy starts inevitably winding down, you need to act on it.

You're already equipped with a natural sense of knowing
when a conversation is winding down.

Here are some universal signs that a conversation is ending and it's time to wrap-up:

- There are longer pauses of silences that don't feel as natural.
- It becomes harder to think of the next thing to say.
- You're not enjoying the conversation as much as you were earlier.
- The other person is giving shorter responses.
- The other person isn't asking questions or introducing new topics.
- The other person is starting to fidget or look around.
- The other person says anything related to needing to leave.

Ignoring these signals and trying to force the conversation past its natural ending can ruin an amazing connection you've just spent your precious time creating. People tend to remember the last feeling you left them with, so you always want to end on a good note.

Just as no one enjoys that one party guest who doesn't know it's time to go home, no one likes being trapped in a conversation with someone who won't take the hint that it's time to end things. Ignoring the connection wind-down signs can also make you seem desperate, which is not exactly the most attractive trait.

I've experienced both sides of the not-knowing-when-to-end-it situation; not only with in-person conversations but over digital communication as well. I've noticed the people who reach out with no real point or purpose ("Hi! How's it going?") tend to be the same ones who don't know when to end that direction-less conversation. So indulging these seemingly innocent, yet totally time-consuming "catch up sessions," also wastes your time trying to then get out of those conversations.

While it's flattering to have someone think of you, it's selfish of them to waste your time by not having – or at least quickly getting to – a point. Speaking from my own perspective, it can feel like they're bored and they want me to entertain them without caring about adding any value to back to me.

Hence the name, "The Catch-Up Cycle of Doom." Conversations like that can continue indefinitely with people you're not close to and be a huge waste of time and energy – and all for no real purpose. Especially when a few repeat offenders keep filling up your inbox.

Creating a deep connection can be so enjoyable that you might be tempted to ignore the "wind-down" signals in favor of keeping those good vibes going just a little bit longer. But trust me, don't do that. Ending a conversation once you sense it's time to do so is always the right choice. Have faith that as long as you practiced the Five Elements of a Meaningful Conversation, your connection went exactly as it was meant to go and if it's in the cards to connect further with the other person, one or both of you will find a way to make it happen.

Your internal knowing of the "wind-down" signal may not be very strong right now, and that's ok. We're not taught how to tune in to the undercurrent of our interactions – but it's never too late to start that awareness. Once you start listening to it, it'll grow stronger and you'll be able to act quickly on it to leave every conversation on a great note and at the right time – which will also leave the other person wanting more of you.

If that connection is with a man you're interested in, go a step further and purposefully end the conversation first. As we covered earlier, people tend to desire what they can't have – especially when it suddenly becomes unavailable to them, which is what happens when you wrap-up a conversation. It will feel empowering for you to end the connection on your terms – especially if you initiated – and know that he'll have to ask you for your phone number to continue it.

Opportunities > Outcomes

There's a lot of information in this chapter, but the premise of how to create a meaningful conversation is simple. Just get curious about the person you're talking to, listen to their answers using mental images, and actively contribute to the conversation with no ulterior motives.

Sometimes the conversation will lead to a date, and sometimes it won't. Release expectations of specific outcomes (e.g. getting a date) because you can't control that – nor can you control the person you're talking to.

> When you bring your genuine self to a connection
> the outcome will be exactly as it was meant to be.

You'll never know the whole story of what's going on with them and what's influencing their decisions in the moment. Maybe they're in the middle of a break-up, maybe they're not attracted to your gender, or maybe they're just having a bad day and don't want to risk feeling even worse if you reject them. Maybe the connection you created was only ever meant to be in that moment, and never intended to go further.

There's incredible freedom in releasing control of the outcome because it means you're only responsible for yourself. Again, who wants the job of being responsible for other people? Still not me.

Ironically, in releasing expectations of a specific outcome and instead focusing on being present in the connection opportunity, you actually *increase* the chance of the right man asking you out.

> Releasing the expectation to achieve a specific outcome
> is more likely to provide that outcome.

People can sense when someone has a hidden agenda, even if not consciously. When you need something from them, it puts them in a position of power – even if they aren't aware of it or choose not to exercise that power.

So instead of worrying mid-conversation if the cute guy you're chatting up at the dog park is going to ask for your phone number, instead shift your focus to being present and enjoying the connection with him. Anything that you try to force in a conversation beyond your half of the conversation risks *decreasing* your chance of getting asked out (unless you feel completely aligned in asking him out yourself, but you already know how I feel about that).

Think of every conversation with a man you're interested in as "practice for the next one," which will shift the focus away from the outcome. That way, each conversation is still serving a purpose – such as fulfilling your need for connection, warming up your skills, and learning more about yourself through another person. Plus that goal will make it easy to have a "successful" conversation every time regardless of what the other person does or doesn't do because that definition of success is entirely about you.

Four Ways to Recover From Forgetting a Name

In *Chapter II: Effortless Engagement*, **you discovered four ways to remember someone's name as soon as they introduce themselves.** But what if you realize halfway through the conversation you've forgotten their name?

Here are four ways to recover a forgotten name…

#1 Be Honest About It

People appreciate honesty, and this can be as simple as, "I'm so sorry, I'm horrible with names. Can you remind me of yours?" The key here is to then go the extra mile to redeem yourself and rebuild the connection that may have just been damaged because you forgot their favorite word. So after they tell you their name again, *repeat it back to them* so they not only get the good feelings associated with hearing it, they see that you're making it a priority to remember it.

#2 Wait for Someone Else to Join

Either wait for or actively bring in someone else to your conversation, so that everyone will re-introduce themselves to the new person. If you know the name of the new person who joined the conversation, introduce *them* to the person whose name you forgot. This will allow the person whose name you forgot to introduce himself back to the new person so you can hear it.

If you don't know the new person who just joined the conversation, simply introduce yourself, then wait for the person whose name you forgot to do the same.

#3 Have Them Add Their Contact Info

If it's the end of the conversation and you want to get together with someone but forgot their name, hand your phone to them and ask them to put their name and number into it. Just make sure you watch to see what their name is before it automatically gets filed into your endless list of contacts. Note: only do this approach if you truly want to get together, because now they're going to be expecting it.

#4 Track Them Down Later

If you have a mutual contact with the person whose name you forgot or if the event you met them at has an attendee list, permission granted to do some stalking by tracking them down any way you can.

Action Item

1. Choose an approach as your go-to method to recover a name:
   #1 Be honest about it.
   #2 Wait for someone else to join.
   #3 Have them add their name and number to your phone.
   #4 Track them down later.

Instant Charm Hacks

"How can you have charisma? Be more concerned about making others feel good about themselves than you are making them feel good about you."
    – Dan Reiland, pastor and leadership coach

The Five Elements of a Meaningful Conversation are your pathway to become genuinely charming in a way that doesn't sacrifice your own enjoyment of the conversation.
    Here are several ways to instantly charm the person you're talking to:

#1 Boost Someone's Ego

Never miss an opportunity to boost someone's ego – whether it's someone you know well or a complete stranger. As with compliments, you'll feel even more joy than the receiver does.

For example, one morning I was hauling a suitcase out of the subway station. It was too big to fit through the turnstile, so I had to use the handicap door to exit. But I could not for the life of me figure out how to get the handicap door to open from the inside. After struggling for a few seconds, a woman walked up and hit the blue "Exit" button that I had somehow completely missed. I said, "You're so smart, thank you!" Just make sure you're not boosting other people's ego at the expense of crushing your own.

#2 Repeat a Key Phrase

You can repeat back a phrase the other person said to incorporate them into your story and/or reaffirm something they said. Just as everyone loves hearing their own name, hearing their own words repeated back to them is right up there as well.

My friend Christie does a great job of this. She's a very eloquent speaker and often pauses when trying to find the perfect words. I know her so well that sometimes I'll jump in with them before she does. If I'm right, she'll nod and repeat them back. For example:

- Christie: *"When she said that to me, it just felt…it just felt…"*
- Me: *"Like she didn't appreciate you?"*
- Christie: *"Exactly. Like she didn't appreciate me. So I asked her …"*

I don't interrupt her flow or turn the conversation back to me; I simply show that I'm following along right there with her.

You can use this technique with strangers too. I was riding in a cab and the driver was from Lagos, Nigeria. We were chatting about being entrepreneurs and he used this "ego boost" technique on me:

- Driver: *"There are a lot of start-up businesses in Lagos."*
- Me: *"I bet – it's the biggest city in Africa!"*
- Driver (slower, emphasizing): *"It's the biggest city in Africa!"*

I could tell he was happy, not just because I knew that fun fact about his hometown, but there was a sense of pride in his tone too. I mean, being from the biggest city on an entire continent is pretty cool.

Of course, don't overuse the "repeat technique," but when you spot an opportunity to wholeheartedly agree with a point someone just made or want to show that you're on the same page, sprinkle it in every now and then.

#3 Revisit These Charm Tips

- *Chapter I: Magnetic Approachability*
  - Open body language (page 43)
  - Make eye contact (page 46)
  - Smile (page 49)
  - Be purposefully playful (page 51)
- *Chapter II: Effortless Engagement*
  - Talk to people as if you're already friends with them (page 60)

- The Five Rules of Engagement when a man talks to you (page 77)
- Eleven ways to break the ice (page 99)
- Four ways to remember someone's name (page 109)
- Add some acknowledgment (page 113)
- *Chapter III: Asked Out Organically*
  - Five Elements of a Meaningful Conversation (page 140)
  - Bridge the gap (page 210)
  - Know when and how to gracefully exit a conversation (page 212)

Action Item

1. Choose one of the charm hacks listed above and apply it in your next conversation.

Ménage à Meaningful

Just like many other introverts, I'm not a "group person." Groups tend to encourage surface-level topics so as to appeal to everyone gathered. Which, for me, means they can feel watered-down and boring.

When I can't avoid being in a group, I make it a goal to find an interesting person and create a one-on-one conversation with them.

If a good connection doesn't happen with that first person (maybe they *are* a "group person"), I'll simply position myself next to someone else and try to connect with them.

You can change-up your position in a group by using an excuse such as ordering food, getting something from your purse, pretending you have to make a call, or going to the restroom. Then, come back to the group and place yourself next to a different person and try to create another connection.

If you're walking in a group, change your position by slowing down or speeding up your pace so you put yourself within proximity of different people. Then use your go-to icebreaker approach from *Chapter II: Effortless*

Engagement to start a conversation and transition into the Five Elements of a Meaningful Conversation to create a connection. Keep shifting around until you find someone you truly click with.

Tech, Interrupted

Sometimes technology will have its way and interrupt an in-person connection. Your phone will ring, ding, or vibrate and you'll feel compelled to look at it. But it's more about how you handle the interruption that matters, which can either strengthen your in-person connection or weaken it.

The key to dealing with a digital disturbance without completely ruining your face-to-face conversation is to always bring that person into your tech conversation. And keep the tech chat as brief as possible.

Let's say you're talking to the man sitting next to you at the airport gate and your phone rings; tell him who it is as soon as you read the name on your screen. If you absolutely have to take the call, keep it short and then debrief him on what the conversation was about afterward. For example:

- Your phone rings.
- You: *"It's my mom calling, one second."*
- (talk to mom for 20 seconds, then hang up)
- You: *"She just wanted to know how to restart her computer. Again. Anyway, what were you saying about that new Gandhi documentary?"*

Including him in that side story will maintain the connection you were building together and allow you to seamlessly pick up where you left off before the disturbance.

When you don't reveal who you're talking to, or provide zero context for your tech conversation, you risk making your in-person person feel instantly excluded and/or that you're hiding something. So, don't do that.

If you receive or have to send a text while in the presence of someone you're talking to, give a short summary of what's going on, so they have context and feel included. Reading your message out loud to them while typing it is a great way to do this. For example:

- *"Please... feed... the... dog..."*
- *"Thanks... for... the... info... talk... later..."*

And of course, another option is to simply keep your phone on silent when you're in a place where you know you'll be connecting with others, so you won't get interrupted in the first place.

CONCLUSION

The World is Now Your Dating Playground

"Opportunities ARE everywhere. Stop playing it so safe and just GO FOR IT. You never know what will happen, who you will meet, or where it could lead...and THAT'S half the fun."
– Dan Meredith, author and entrepreneur

And that's a wrap! You now have a shiny new toolbox full of tips, techniques, and examples of how to attract a great man in the real world, and live a more fulfilling life in general.

There's a lot of information in this book, but remember you only need to apply a few tips at a time to start seeing great results in your own life.

The most important factor is that you take action. Any action. Start with the Action Items sprinkled throughout the pages, or with practicing your eye contact skills, or pushing past your fear of awkward silences, or sharing something personal with a stranger to deepen that connection.

I understand trying new things can feel scary. Over the years, I've pushed myself to make very uncomfortable changes in my life such as:

- Moving to six different cities by myself.
- Quitting an unsatisfying job without having another one lined up.
- Starting my own business.
- Ending longstanding-turned-toxic friendships.
- Breaking up with men I loved because they weren't right for me.

The hardest part of adopting a new way of interacting with others is taking that very first step to get your momentum going.

I encourage you to start with one tip from this book. Just one. And try it out a few times. Then choose another tip and try that out a few times. I guarantee if you take this "one tip at a time" approach, you'll start creating incredible new connections.

It's like learning to drive: the methods might feel foreign at first, but with a little practice they'll become like second nature. I've even had clients share that they forgot what their life was like before gaining their connection superpowers – and after only a few weeks of applying the techniques.

Your future guy is out there, right now, looking for you too. All it takes is one word, or even a smile, to spark a new connection with a man – or *anyone* – who can change your entire life.

Now, go get 'em girl!

A One-Minute Way to Help Women Around the World

If you enjoyed The Offline Dating Method, I'd appreciate if you could take one minute to add a five-star review of the book on Amazon.com to help get this book into the hands of other women who are struggling in their love lives. Leaving a positive review shows them that this book is worth their time and money, and the tips can help them ditch the digital dating scene and start attracting great men in the real world.

COACHING

How to Upgrade Your Support

"The single most important element in developing an expertise is your willingness to practice."
– Gretchen Rubin, *The Happiness Project*

How strange that choosing a life partner is arguably the most important decision of our lives, yet one of which we invest the least.

If after applying some of the tips you're feeling overwhelmed or like you could use some extra support on your journey to meeting a great guy in the real world, I invite you to check out my group coaching program The Offline Dating Academy and one-on-one private coaching program Confidence Connection Commitment.

With both programs, you will have direct access to me, and we'll tailor the approaches to fit you and your lifestyle. I'll be by your side to support you every step of the way as you work toward reaching your dating and relationship goals.

Confidence Connection Commitment
Private one-on-one coaching with Camille Virginia
Go to **www.MasterOfflineDating.com/Coaching**

*"I found a **new best friend and terrific relationship**. Camille encouraged me to be myself with men and coached me through the stages of friendship to relationship, and was my sounding board when I played mind games with myself. **I give her all the credit for the best relationship I have ever had**."*
– Mary, my client

The Offline Dating Academy
Group coaching program led by Camille Virginia
www.MasterOfflineDating.com/Academy

"Working with Camille has been life-transforming, not only with dating but in interacting with the world around me. I'm really glad I joined The Academy."

– Eileen, Academy member

If coaching isn't for you right now, I invite you to grab my FREE gift, The Offline Dating Method Experiential Workbook. It contains all Action Items from this book in one convenient resource, as well as dozens of exclusive bonus exercises not found in the book so you can apply the material easier.

The Offline Dating Method FREE Experiential Workbook

Grab it at: www.OfflineDatingMethod.com

No need to cull through this entire book trying to find your notes; the workbook helps keep you organized and on track to attract great men in the real world.

With the workbook also comes complimentary access to The Offline Dating Challenge: 3 Days to a Red-Hot Date in the Real World, which sends key tips from each chapter straight to your inbox as you read The Offline Dating Method.

Don't let all this invaluable material disappear as soon as you close this book. Results like attracting great men and creating deeper relationships only come with consistent action, so why not make taking action as easy as possible?

The Sequel and The Prequel

Now that you know how to attract great men into your life, how do you know which man is the right one for you? Or turn your meaningful connection into a romantic one? Or navigate from the first date to an actual relationship?

The three chapters of this book are only three steps of my signature system The Offline Dating Method. The full nine-step framework goes beyond the meaningful connection material we covered in this book...

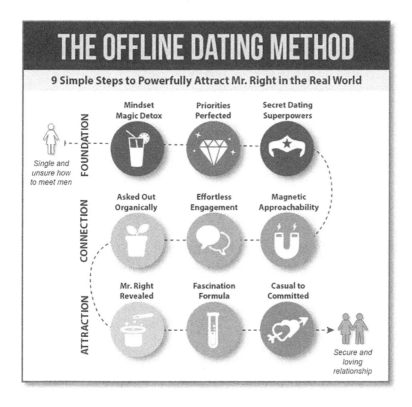

The nine steps include how to live a quality life surrounded by great people, how to tap into your femininity, how to unlock your natural flirt style, how to fall in love with yourself (so the right man naturally will too), how to make sure you choose the right man, and more.

After going through all nine steps, you'll have everything you need to be your best self and live your best life with the man of your dreams.

In my next book, *Find Love Offline* (coming Fall 2020), I'll show you how to take the meaningful connections you've created in *The Offline Dating Method* and turn them into a passionate romantic connection…

Find Love Offline
The Sequel to *The Offline Dating Method*
(coming Fall 2020)

Chapter I: Mr. Right Revealed
Receive crystal clarity on the right man so you never fall for the wrong one again

- **Clarify + Qualify: 2 Secret Moves to Reveal Your Mr. Right**
  - Three Levels of Crystal Clarity
  - Three Points of Qualification

- **Attraction Tips to Make Sure He's Mr. Right**
  - Be Open to a Different Package
  - Where to Meet Men
  - Glaring Red Flags
  - Make Space For Him

Chapter II: Fascination Formula
Unlock your feminine assets to completely captivate him and deepen his desire

- **Femininity 101: Harness the Power of Your Softer Side**
  - Masculinity + Mixed Messages
  - Find Your Balance
  - Six Ways to Shift Into Your Feminine

- Flirting 101: Unlock Your Natural Attraction Tool
  - Here's What Flirting is NOT
  - What's Your Natural Flirting Style?
  - Flirting: What to Say
  - Flirting: What To Do

Chapter III: Casual To Committed
Navigate from the first date into your own magical happily-ever-after together

- Dating Phase No-No's: Avoid These Actions at All Costs
- The Three Phases of Dating
  - 1) How to Have the Best First Date EVER
  - 2) How to Navigate the Second Date Onward
  - 3) Have to Approach the DTR ("Define the Relationship") Talk

Book #3 (title to be determined)
The Prequel to *The Offline Dating Method*
(coming 2021)

Chapter I: Mindset Magic Detox
Melt away toxic thought patterns and create a clear path to the love you deserve

- Two Types of Toxic Mindset Barriers
  - Internal Mindset Barriers
  - External Mindset Barriers
- Three Stages of Mindset Magic Detox
  - 1) Awareness: Diagnose the Situation
  - 2) Appreciation: Love it and leave it
  - 3) Antidote: Create your new healthy habit

Chapter II: Priorities Perfected

Boost self-confidence by downsizing your commitments and upgrading your life

- **Five Phases of Building Your Awesome New Life**
  - 1) Assess: Reveal who + what you're prioritizing
  - 2) Accept: Say it with me now
  - 3) Aspire: Dream big – and then dream bigger
  - 4) Adios: Send-off stuff no longer serving you
  - 5) Align: Design Your Life to Support Your Dreams

Chapter III: Secret Dating Superpowers

Cultivate a sexy strong sense of self to feel unwavering worthiness of a great guy

- **Unlocking Your Four Secret Superpowers**
  - #1 Personality: Working with your innate wiring
  - #2 Hobbies + Interests: Recreation on your road to purpose
  - #3 Values: Your core drivers for... well, everything
  - #4 Passions + Purpose: Your fulfilling contribution to the world

---

Be first to grab *Find Love Offline*

Want to get the inside scoop on my next book *Find Love Offline* and be first to hear when it hits the shelves?

Go to **www.OfflineDatingMethod.com/NextBooks** to stay up to date on all things offline dating - including free resources, bonus tips, and so much more.

ACKNOWLEDGMENTS

A Few Special Thank-You's

This book happened with the support of many people, and I'd like to give a personal shout-out those who helped make it possible.

To my parents, **Ed** and **Peggy**, thank you for being incredibly supportive of me and my sometimes-unconventional life choices – like quitting the corporate world to start my own business, moving across the country multiple times (sometimes in the same month), and a few "Are you sure about this?" decisions on the romance front (that turned into priceless lessons!). You've had my back every step of the way and I love you.

To my publisher **Jesse Krieger**, for selecting my book proposal as the contest winner and gifting me a full publishing package, which is what helped bring this book into the world. Thank you also for your patience in working with a Type-A perfectionist who was brand new to the publishing process by indulging my endless edits, requests, and questions along the way.

To my publicist **Laura Gianino**, who shares not only my passion for human connection but also attention to detail. Thank you for working tirelessly to get this book into the hands of media everywhere and helping spread the message of meaningful connection.

To my early readers, who contributed supportive feedback, detailed edits, and thoughtful reviews for this book. Thank you for helping make it the best it could be: **Alison Suell, Diana Tower, Jeffrey Kahrs, John Moenk, Julia Willard, Margaret Winn, Mary Ellen, Melody DiCroce, Saba, Shelyna Brown, Varvara Mokeeva, Zelda Benson**, and **Zenna**.

To **all my friends** who encouraged and supported me throughout this journey, you know I love you.

To **Anne** and **Sarika** for that fateful night in May 2013 when you asked me to create a PowerPoint on how to meet men in the real world. Who knew that little eight-slide presentation would turn into three books and a business reaching women in over 100 different countries!

To my friend and fellow dating coach **Jason Silver** who has been an endless source of encouragement and loving nudges to go to the next levels in my coaching business.

To **Ariadne Ducas** for being my constant cheerleader through every step of our parallel adventures in life, love, and entrepreneurship.

To **all my clients and readers**, thank you for allowing me to support you and share your stories, and for helping hone my methods and material. Whether you attended a workshop (held in my tiny Chicago apartment back in the day), joined one of my courses, coached with me, or simply reached out with a kind word about how I or my content has impacted you, please know I am grateful for you.

I'd also like to thank **you, dear reader**, for investing your time and money in this book. I hope it gives you the superpowers to attract amazing people of all relationship types and to lead a more fulfilling life in general.

And lastly, to **every man I've ever dated**: thank you for the clarity on what I want (and don't want) in a partner, and for your contribution to these epic stories, invaluable lessons, and wonderful adventures.

GUIDE

All Book Sections by Page Number

Introduction: Your Secret Edge Over the Apps 1
- The Five Digital Barriers Keeping You Single............................ 2
- The Solution is Simple 4
- The Journey That Led Me to You 8
- The Universal Power of Human Connection.............................. 9
- Your Roadmap to Real-World Connection 9
- How to Avoid "Advice Overwhelm" 10
- A Special Invitation 11

Chapter I: Magnetic Approachability...................... 13
- Results You'll Get From This Chapter 16
- The Irresistible Woman: Authentic, Alluring, *Approachable* ... 17
  - Location is Everything 18
  - Simple Social Warm-Ups...20
    - #1 The Value of Volunteering.......................................20
    - #2 The Vacation Mindset..21
    - #3 Alone = Approachable..21
    - #4 The 20-Minute Trick..22
  - The #1 Principle of Approachability.....................................24
  - Seven Ways to Snap Into the Present....................................25
    - #1 Meditate 25
    - #2 Capture Your Thoughts...25
    - #3 Notice Your Breath...26
    - #4 Indulge Your Senses...26
    - #5 People-Watch 26

- #6 Acknowledge Someone...27
- #7 Paint a Mental Picture 27
- **Three Pillars of Magnetic Approachability 28**
  - Pillar 1: Prepping 29
    - #1 Set a Powerful Intention 29
    - #2 Dress for Confidence + a Conversation 30
      - Dress for Confidence 31
        - i. Boost your confidence 31
        - ii. Harness the power of another persona 32
        - iii. Show respect for yourself and others...........................34
      - Dress for a Conversation 35
        - i. Make a (silent) personal statement 35
        - ii. Attract like-minded people 36
        - iii. Get noticed naturally 36
          - Mismatch your environment..37
          - Leave your name tag on 37
          - Step up + dress up 37
  - Pillar 2: Positioning 39
    - #1 Case the Joint..39
      - Be prepared, not scared...40
      - Use your peripheral powers 40
    - #2 Scout Your Spot..41
  - Pillar 3: Projecting 43
    - #1 Keep a Headphone Out 43
    - #2 Body Language Basics 43
      - i. Imaginary Party Trick 44
      - ii. Mental body scan...44
      - iii. Open yourself up to the world..................................45
      - iv. Secretly synchronize 45
    - #3 Flash a Sexy Glance..46
      - i. Check out the space..47
      - ii. Have a virtual staring contest 47
      - iii. Note his eye color..48
      - iv. "Looking for someone?"..48
      - v. Challenge your limit...48
      - vi. Practice in groups 48

- #4 Prevent "Resting Bitch Face" (in one quick move)......................49
  - i. The Secret Smile..49
  - ii. Become a Mouth Breather 49
- #5 Start "Squinching" 50
- #6 Be Purposefully Playful..51
- #7 Let Him Do It..52

Chapter II: Effortless Engagement 55
- Results You'll Get From This Chapter 60
- Consistency 101: Your Shift into Effortless Engagement 65
  - Here's Why We're Inconsistent...66
  - The Instant Cure for Inconsistency 67
    - The Ellen Effect 68
  - But "Consistency" is NOT This… 69
  - Two Aspects of Consistency 71
    - #1 The Script is the Same 71
      - Assume everyone gets your awesome sense of humor..............72
    - #2 Set + Keep a Similar Tone 74
  - Important Note on Cultural Differences....................................75
- If He Initiates With You… 77
  - The Rules of Engagement...77
    - Rule #1: Assume He's Interested 77
    - Rule #2: Find the Positive 78
    - Rule #3: Accept All Compliments..80
    - Rule #4: Just Go With It 82
      - Embrace the "Yes, and…" 83
    - Rule #5: Don't Be Cruel..85
- If You Initiate With Him… 87
  - The Rules of Engagement...87
    - Rule #1: You Can Totally Initiate..87
    - Rule #2: Choose Easy + Relatable 88
    - Rule #3: Skip the Formalities..89
    - Rule #4: Opportunity > Outcome 90
    - Rule #5: Prepare For Rain..92
  - Overcoming the Four Fears 92

- Fear of Rejection...94
- Fear of Being Awkward 96
- Fear of Being Creepy...97
- Fear He's Already Taken...97
- Eleven Super Simple Ways to Start a Conversation...................99
  - #1 Pull a RAOK..99
  - #2 Drop a Compliment..100
  - #3 Change It Up...100
  - #4 Casually Cut-In...101
  - #5 Sprinkle Some Value 102
  - #6 Share a Short Quip 102
  - #7 Spread the News 103
  - #8 Try a "Hi"..103
  - #9 Ask a Question..104
  - #10 Put In a Request...105
  - #11 Make Someone Smile 105
- How to Keep it Going – Or Shut It Down 106
  - The Four-Word Transition to Meaningful...........................106
  - Death of a Conversation...107
- Essential Engagement Extras 109
  - Four Ways to Never Forget Someone's Name Again 109
    - #1 Associate It With Someone You Know (or Know of) 110
    - #2 Visualize It Spelled Out 110
    - #3 Repeat it Right Back..111
    - #4 Create a Convention 111
  - Nine Actions to Gain Social Momentum 112
    - #1 Add Some Acknowledgment 113
    - #2 Say It Out Loud 114
    - #3 Do a Drive-By 114
    - #4 Be in Movement 116
    - #5 Phone a Friend...116
    - #6 Play The Rejection Game...116
    - #7 Do a Live Video 117
    - #8 Go to Conferences and Events 117
    - #9 Practice with Everyone 118

- How to Handle "One of Those Days" 119

Chapter III: Asked Out Organically 121
- Results You'll Get From This Chapter 125
  - Instant Results 125
  - Lifelong Results 132
- Warning! You'll Be a Wanted Woman 135
  - How to Avoid The Catch-Up Cycle of Doom........................136
  - All Praise and No Action Makes Anyone a Dull Boy (or Girl)....139
- The Five Elements of a Meaningful Conversation................. 140
  - Recap: The Four-Word Transition to Meaningful 141
  - Your Biggest Fears Are Your Biggest Opportunities.................141
  - Element 1: Ask Awesome Questions 142
    - Say It Like You Mean It 143
    - Be Authentically Curious 145
    - Ask Questions You Want Asked Back to You 146
    - Go for Depth, Not Breadth 147
    - List: Best Types of Questions 149
  - Element 2: Hold Space for Silence................................150
  - Element 3: Listen Like Your Life Depends Upon It 152
    - The Empathic Listening Technique 153
      - How to create on-demand experiences 155
      - ELT Example #1: Hiking Mount Everest.....................157
      - ELT Example #2: Lunch date with a friend................160
      - The Empathic Listening Technique is doable..............162
      - Two Bonuses of The Empathic Listening Technique 163
      - Disclaimer: Watch out for these topics 163
    - Acknowledge Without Interrupting 164
      - Here's why people interrupt.....................................164
        - #1 You want to show you're listening 165
        - #2 You get genuinely excited and inspired to contribute........165
        - #3 You want to share your insight before you forget it 165
        - #4 You think you know what they're going to say 166
        - #5 You want to turn the topic back to you 166
      - The Interruption Remedy 167

- • If you're the cut-off culprit 167
  - • Dealing with a serial interrupter 167
- • Loosen Your Grip..168
- • Element 4: Release Judgment 169
  - • Note: You *Will* Judge 170
  - • Two Ways Fear of Judgment Manifests..............................171
    - • #1 When you *decide* what others are thinking..............171
    - • #2 When you're *dependent on* what others are thinking 173
  - • The (Surprising) Root of All Judgment..............................173
  - • Three Steps to Stop Judging..175
    - • 1) Catch it + go deeper 175
    - • 2) Channel into curiosity, a compliment, or compassion 176
    - • 3) Rinse and repeat..177
  - • Why Your Words Are a Mirror 179
  - • Be Open Past the First Impression 180
- • Element 5: Share Insights and Stories 182
  - • The Crucial Benefits of Contributing to the Conversation 184
  - • How to Comfortably Contribute 187
    - • #1 Create a repertoire of your favorite topics and stories..........187
    - • #2 Gather daily insights and personal anecdotes 188
    - • #3 Create a purposeful juxtaposition..............................189
    - • #4 Humanize yourself 191
    - • #5 Aim for concepts, not people 193
    - • #6 Show, don't tell 193
    - • #7 Take someone back to the moment 194
    - • #8 Ask questions that you want to be asked back to you 195
    - • #9 Talk about the future..195
  - • Declining a Question 196
  - • Contributing vs Bragging 197
- • How to Seal the Deal 199
- • Here's Why It Needs to Be an Actual Date..............................199
- • Three Ways to Get a Date with Him..200
  - • #1 Inspire Him to Ask You Out..200
    - • Give him an extra second – literally..............................201
    - • It may be subtle..202
  - • #2 Put the Ball in His Court..203

- #3 Ask Him Out 206
- Script: How I Got a Date on LinkedIn..............................206
- **More Tips for Your Conversational Arsenal** **208**
  - Don't Say This to Him, or Anyone. Ever.........................208
    - #1 Don't Be a Meanie..209
    - #2 Start Light on the Intensity 210
    - #3 Bridge the Gap (Don't Deepen the Divide) 210
    - #4 No Self-Deprecation, Please. Thanks. 211
  - How to Know When to Exit the Conversation 212
  - Opportunities > Outcomes...214
  - Four Ways to Recover From Forgetting a Name.............216
    - #1 Be Honest About It...216
    - #2 Wait for Someone Else to Join 217
    - #3 Have Them Add Their Contact Info 217
    - #4 Track Them Down Later 217
  - Instant Charm Hacks 218
    - #1 Boost Someone's Ego..218
    - #2 Repeat a Key Phrase 218
    - #3 Revisit These Charm Tips 219
  - Ménage à Meaningful..220
  - Tech, Interrupted 221

Conclusion: The World is Now Your Dating Playground... **223**

Coaching: How to Upgrade Your Support.............. **225**

Next Books: The Sequel and The Prequel **227**

Acknowledgments: A Few Special Thank-You's...... **233**

Guide: All Book Sections by Page Number **237**

Index **245**

Index

20-Minute Trick, The, 22

acknowledgment, 39, 92, 113, 152

Action Items, 18, 23, 28, 29, 34, 38, 52,
71, 76, 82, 98, 106, 107, 109, 112,
118, 139, 149, 162, 167, 179, 183,
188, 210, 217, 220

advice overwhelm (how to avoid), 10

alter-ego phenomenon, 33

anecdotes (see also *stories*), 188, 189

Anti-Judgment Loop, 175, 178

appreciation, 9, 27, 75, 83, 152, 166,
198

approachability, 14-52, 219

Aron, Dr. Arthur, 5, 46, 126

awkward (fear of being), 96-97

awkward silence, 125, 150-151, 209

body language, 5, 7, 30, 43-45

bragging, 62, 182, 192, 194, 197-198

breaking the ice, 71, 87-105

Catch-Up Cycle of Doom, The, 136-
138, 214

charm, 218-220

clothing (and accessories), 30-38

comfort zone, 21, 22, 48, 91, 161

compassion, 143, 169, 175-179, 185

compatibility, 7, 40, 182-183, 185

compliments, 27, 35, 59, 80-81, 100, 105,
107, 114-116, 119, 141, 169, 175-177,
218

accepting, 80-81

Compliment Drive-By, 114-116, 119

compliments (*cont.*)

Compliment Rampage, 115

giving, 20, 21, 48, 60, 65, 81, 92, 114,
137, 144, 147, 150, 152, 166, 191,
194, 198, 206, 212, 213

confidence:

conversation, 56, 107

dressing for, 30-34, 36, 78, 82, 176,
189

self, 49, 123

social, 28-38

consistency, 65-74

contribution (to conversation), 90,
139, 165, 182-198

control (of conversation), 62, 89, 91,
168, 215

conversations:

creating a safe space, 17, 24, 39, 129,
159, 164, 169, 203

draining, 58, 66, 122, 162

ending / exiting, 107-108, 212-214

energizing (make), 125

small talk, 58, 62, 106, 122-123, 150,
169

transition into meaningful, 106-107,
141

creepy, 52, 83, 93, 97, 206

fear of being, 35, 39, 93, 97

cultural differences, 75-76

curiosity, 143-146, 169, 175-177,
186

date:
    how to get one, 200-206
    importance of an actual, 199-200
Digital Barriers (Five), 2-4
Digital Minimalism (Newport), 135
Elements of a Meaningful
    Conversation (Five), The 140-198
    Element 1, 142-149
    Element 2, 150-151
    Element 3, 152-168
    Element 4, 169-181
    Element 5, 182-198
Ellen Effect, The, 68-69
Emotional Labor, 57-60
Empathic Listening Technique, The
    131-132, 153-163, 165
epiphanies, 128, 129, 131, 153, 156,
    165
eye contact, 24, 27, 40, 46-49, 91, 113,
    151, 167, 223
fear:
    he's already taken, 93, 97-98
    of being awkward, 93, 96-97
    of being creepy, 35, 39, 93, 97
    of judgment, 171-173
    of rejection, 1, 10, 16, 17, 21, 61, 89,
        93-96, 116, 128, 201, 202, 203
filtering / screen (out wrong people),
    5, 126, 128, 173, 184, 185
*Five Keys of Mindful Communication,
    The* (Gillis Chapman), 24, 169
formalities, 87, 89-90
Four-Word Transition to Meaningful,
    106-107, 141
Fried Green Tomatoes, 212
Friendly or Flirting Technique, 94-96
fulfillment, 1, 4, 7, 122, 134, 163

Galinsky, Dr. Adam, 31
gossip, 193
Gottman, Dr. John, 64
group:
    activity, 20
    conversations in a, 48, 220
    of people, 16, 21, 48, 220
Happiness Project, The (Rubin), 225
he's already taken (fear), 93, 97-98
headphones, 43, 52
Hochschild, Arlie, 57
honesty, 5, 108, 171, 216
*How to Win Friends and Influence
    People* (Carnegie), 109
humor (see *sense of humor*)
*I Suck at Relationships So You Don't
    Have To* (Frankel), 196
icebreakers, 36, 42, 72, 81, 88-89, 99-
    105, 116, 181, 220
    eleven super simple, 99-105
Imaginary Party Trick, 44
impression (on others), 6, 30, 34-35,
    58, 67, 74, 180-181, 182, 187, 191
inconsistency, 67-70
insecurity, 131, 174-175, 178, 192, 198,
    211-212
insights, 11, 25, 128-130, 137, 139,
    144-145, 164-165, 170, 182-196
intention:
    behind words, 57, 76, 78, 85, 98, 104,
        127, 130, 143, 144, 169, 196-198
    setting an, 29
interrupting:
    acknowledge without, 164-168
    how to stop, 167-168
    why people do it, 164-166
invisible to men, 16

judgment, 27, 73, 122, 169-181
  Anti-Judgment Loop, 178
  fear of, 171-173
  Judgment Loop, 174-175
  root of, 173-174
  three steps to stop, 175-179
  using best, 76
juxtaposition, 189, 190
kindness, 7, 35, 92, 144, 177, 212
  random act of (RAOK), 99, 115
LinkedIn ask-out, 206-207
listening skills, 122, 130, 132, 152-168,
  202, 210
locations (to meet men), 18-19
loneliness, 1, 135, 147
Magnetic Approachability (state of),
  15, 16, 20, 28, 29
Make Every Man Want You (Forleo), 152
Maslow's Hierarchy of Needs, 15, 56,
  123
meditation, 25
Mind to Mouth Move, 96, 102
missed opportunities, 60, 61, 181, 202,
  218
Modern Romance (Ansari), 2
momentum, 112-118, 223
  nine actions to get into social, 112-
  118
name tags, 37, 113
names, 98, 114, 221
  how to recover forgotten, 216-217
  how to remember, 109-111
neural pathway, 175, 177
neuroplasticity, 175
online dating, 2, 3, 4, 6, 8
overthinking, 71
Paradox of Choice, The (Schwartz), 2

parameters, 194
people-watching, 26, 39
peripheral vision, 40-41
Pillars of Magnetic Approachability
  (three), 28-52
  Pillar 1, 29-38
  Pillar 2, 39-42
  Pillar 3, 43-52
playfulness, 51-52, 149, 202
praise, 139-140
present (being), 24-27, 29, 113, 122,
  125, 131, 152, 153, 154, 168, 188,
  215, 216
  importance of, 24-25
  seven ways to snap into, 25-27
Pride and Prejudice (2005), 77
Principle of Approachability (#1), 24
questions:
  as icebreaker, 20, 95, 101, 104-105,
    117, 168
  as part of meaningful conversation,
    122, 126, 128, 130-131, 140, 142-
    149, 154-159, 161, 167, 195, 206
  asking for context, 78-79, 154-159,
    167
  decline answering, 196-197
  great / best ones to ask, 129, 143,
    145-147,149, 156, 157, 159, 195
  to keep conversation going, 81, 90,
    141, 152
quotes:
  Achor, Shawn, 185
  Angelou, Dr. Maya, 123
  Ansari, Aziz, 2
  Ardeleanu, Sorinne, 59
  Aron, Dr. Arthur, 46
  Aslay, Jonathon, 140

quotes (*cont.*)

Batiste, Jon, 113
Blankl, Jennifer, 114
Borge, Victor, 72
Brown, Dr. Brené, 182
Carnegie, Dale, 109
Chapman, Susan Gillis, 24, 169
Cicero, 150
Covey, Dr. Stephen, 64
Dahl, Roald, 49
DeGeneres, Ellen, 68
Dr. Seuss, 173
Edge, Steve, 35
Emerson, Ralph Waldo, 142
Fields, Rachel, 66
Ford, Arielle, 11
Forleo, Marie, 152
Frankel, Bethenny, 196
Gilad, Adam, 51
Graves, Ginny, 30
Halpern, Derek, 36
Harbinger, AJ, 191
Herman, Todd, 31, 32
Hesse, Hermann, 173
Hurley, Peter, 50
Hussey, Matthew, 62
Jimmy Eat World, 197
Katz, Evan Marc, 17
Kerr, Robert, 176
Krieger, Jesse, 94
Macapinlac, Myke, 139
Meredith, Dan, 223
Myers, David, 210
Newport, Cal, 135
Perel, Esther, 128
Reiland, Dan, 218
Roosevelt, Eleanor, 193
Rowley, Cynthia, 31

quotes (*cont.*)

Rubin, Gretchen, 225
Sax, David, 4
Seneca, 90
Swift, Taylor, 18
Van Ness, Jonathan, 75
Waters, Story, 170
Weiss, Suzannah, 57
Yeats, William Butler, 67
ZZ Top, 30
random act of kindness (RAOK), 99, 115
rapport (building), 62, 68, 111, 127
rejection:
    fear of, 1, 10, 16, 17, 21, 61, 89, 93-96, 116, 128, 201, 202, 203
    risk of, 16, 17, 21, 61, 87, 89, 203
Rejection Therapy, 116
Rejection Game, The, 116
respect, 7, 34, 97, 98, 113, 123
"Resting Bitch Face," 49
results (to expect in chapter):
    Chapter I, 16-17
    Chapter II, 60-65
    Chapter III, 125-135
Revenge of Analog, The (Sax), 4
Rules of Engagement, The:
    if he initiates, 77-86
    if you initiate, 87-92
Runaway Bride, 65
scan (new environment), 39, 40, 41, 85
Schumer, Amy, 80
scout (your spot), 41-42
selective (how to be), 126, 136
self-deprecation, 73, 80, 193, 211-212
sense of humor, 35, 72-74, 78, 84, 86, 102, 188, 210
Sharing Spectrum, The, 183-184, 198

shyness, 8, 9, 20, 35, 47, 60, 91, 192, 199, 204

silence:

avoiding awkward, 125, 168, 209, 213

holding space for, 140, 150-151, 198

"Situationship," 199

Small Talk Trap, The, 58, 122

smiling, 25, 27, 29, 49-50, 51, 75, 91, 103, 105, 116, 168, 197, 224

social momentum (see *momentum*)

Social Psychology (Myers), 210

squinching, 50-51

stories:

asking for context, 78-79, 154-159, 167

creating / sharing / contributing to, 27, 81, 123, 127, 130, 131-132, 137, 145, 153, 156, 161, 167, 182, 193-195, 218

repertoire of, 187-188

storytime, 154-155

technology, 1, 2, 4, 14, 58, 206, 221-221

Ten-Five Rule, 113

tone (of voice), 62, 67-69, 71, 74-75, 89, 144, 191, 206

total recall, 131-132

trust / trustworthiness, 5, 62, 69, 75, 76, 96, 127-128, 151, 164

Twits, The (Dahl), 49

Vacation Mindset, The, 21

validation, 64, 65, 73, 139, 166, 182-183, 187, 191-193, 197-198, 212

visual listening (see *Empathic Listening Technique*)

volunteering, 20, 102

vulnerability, 62, 169, 182, 185-187, 191-192

where to meet men (see *locations*)

wind down (a conversation), 212-214

"Yes, and…," 83-85

Zone of Hospitality, The, 113

CPSIA information can be obtained
at www.ICGtesting.com
Printed in the USA
LVHW061533011019
632803LV00016B/723/P